MW00784535

COLORADO'S
HISTORIC
HOTELS

COLORADO'S HISTORIC HOTELS

Alexandra Walker Clark

Charleston — London

THE
History
PRESS

Published by The History Press
Charleston, SC 29403
www.historypress.net

Copyright © 2011 by Alexandra Walker Clark
All rights reserved

First published 2011

Manufactured in the United States

ISBN 978.1.60949.301.1

Library of Congress Cataloging-in-Publication Data

Clark, Alexandra Walker.
Colorado's historic hotels / Alexandra Walker Clark.
p. cm.
ISBN 978-1-60949-301-1
1. Hotels--Colorado--History. 2. Historic buildings--Colorado. 3. Architecture--Colorado--
History. 4. Colorado--History, Local. 5. Colorado--Biography. I. Title.
TX909.C53 2011
917.8806--dc23
2011018251

Notice: The information in this book is true and complete to the best of our knowledge. It is
offered without guarantee on the part of the author or The History Press. The author and
The History Press disclaim all liability in connection with the use of this book.

All rights reserved. No part of this book may be reproduced or transmitted in any form
whatsoever without prior written permission from the publisher except in the case of
brief quotations embodied in critical articles and reviews.

For Wendell C. Walker,
who taught me the love of western travel.

With special thanks to:

Elizabeth Dixon
Coy Gehrig, Denver Public Library
Becky Le Jeune
Liam Moskowitz
Jeff Christlieb
Bill Moskowitz, Road Warrior

CONTENTS

INTRODUCTION

For more than 150 years, Colorado has beckoned, and people have responded, some drawn to its beauty, some seeking fortune and some hoping to reclaim health. Colorado has welcomed them all—proud and wealthy, humble and hopeful—extending its majestic arms to incomers of every stripe. Even before the silver booms and gold rushes that built the mining towns, people came to discover Colorado's high peaks, the healing waters of its abundant hot springs and its rich hunting and fishing resources.

Some were drawn by the earth itself, seeking land to develop agriculturally. Many ranches began to promote their properties as guest ranches to compete with hotels and boardinghouses. Enter the early version of the dude ranch.

The nineteenth century was a time of building, of breaking new ground. Settlements were established on the windblown plains and above timberline. The promise of new land and its opportunities brought to Colorado those who scarcely could afford to risk their futures, yet they were not timid or afraid of work. These were miners, cowhands, laborers—risking all for the chance to better their lives. They were settlers, tourists and fortune-seekers, and a more diverse lot could not have been gathered. But they all needed shelter.

Enter the modest entrepreneur. These lodge keepers seldom had great means, yet they were willing to risk it all. Some might have obtained loans from obliging banks, monies that they sank into modest hotels or boardinghouses in hopes of becoming successful business owners. A surprising number of these were women, often widowed or unmarried, who seized the opportunity to establish themselves on par with male counterparts. To own a hotel was to demand respect—not an abundant commodity for women in those days, even back East.

Sometimes a husband and wife might make such a venture together, and as their enterprise succeeded, they would acquire a second hotel, the man running one operation and his wife the other. In these challenging circumstances, families had to stick together.

Note: An asterisk by listing indicates businesses still in operation.

Eastern Counties

Eastern Colorado seldom drew people for its scenic beauty, as did the mountains and hot springs. While those who settled the plains were primarily farmers and ranchers, there were also businessmen, who saw an opportunity to operate stores and offer services. Every new business drew drummers, or traveling salesmen, who required rooms for themselves and their wares. With the smaller communities' growth came the need for teachers and other professionals, who also required temporary housing.

Hotels struggled on this meager fare, and many did not last long. The settlers and businesses that did survive in eastern Colorado heroically battled drought, heat, isolation, ravenous insects, frequent tornados and the housekeeper's bane, warm Chinook winds that repeatedly blew fine layers of dust into every crevice. But the people of eastern Colorado are a hardy lot, and their perseverance has paid off in the permanent communities that today dot the plains like welcome oases.

Baca County

Baca County was created by the Colorado legislature in 1889 from portions of Las Animas County. It is in the southernmost eastern corner of the state, named for Colorado territorial legislator Felipe Baca.

Springfield

Springfield began officially on April 12, 1887, so named because most of its residents had lived in Springfield, Missouri. One of the first commissioners was Frank Tipton, whose original eighty acres are believed to have been the original town site. With the establishment of a courthouse, a jail (mostly for horse thieves) was required.

For some $3,000, the town constructed a two-cell steel cage. The jail opened for business in 1889, and it was reported that the sheriff could not exceed ninety-five cents for feeding prisoners. The area's main crime was horse stealing. The reward for apprehending a horse thief was $25, until one citizen led a campaign to raise that amount to $100 due to the significantly rising number of stolen horses.

Other than that, Springfield was generally quiet, and sometimes a week might pass without anyone coming into town. Storekeepers often stayed at home until a potential customer came into view.

Springfield is located in the southeast corner of the state and is an agricultural community.

JONES HOTEL: Located on Main Street, the Jones Hotel was built prior to 1913.

Main Street, Springfield, Colorado. A newspaper office next to the two-story Jones Hotel, 1913.

Cheyenne County

The present boundaries of Cheyenne County were established in 1889. It was named for the area's original residents, the Cheyenne Indians, who occupied eastern Colorado before it was settled by whites.

Wild Horse

This town is named for the herds of wild horses that once thundered across these plains, watering at nearby Wild Horse Creek. The entire town burned down in 1917 but was partially rebuilt.

A postcard of Wild Horse, Colorado, in 1917, shortly before the town fire that same year. The Albany Hotel is the stone structure on the right at center.

ALBANY HOTEL: Located on Main Street, the Albany Hotel was built prior to 1917. It was razed by the town fire in 1917. PFALTZGRAFF HOTEL: Built by William H. Pfaltzgraff, this hotel burned down in 1917.

Kiowa County

Kiowa County was established in 1889, named for the Kiowa Nation. Kiowa County is the site of the infamous Sand Creek Massacre on November 29, 1864, in which a Kiowa settlement of old men, women and children were ruthlessly slaughtered on Sand Creek by U.S. forces. Initially hailed as a victory against hostile Indians, within months, congressional inquiries disclosed the outrage that still remains a dark blot on the nation's historical record.

The 1930s Dust Bowl reduced eastern Colorado's agriculture to the precarious conditions of today. While the land still supports some dry land farming and ranching, upstream interests have acquired most of the water rights, and the aquifers are drying up. If this trend continues, Kiowa County could one day revert to its original grassland and prairie state.

Brandon: Essentially a Ghost Town

Established in 1887, Brandon became a busy trade center. But the Dust Bowl took its toll, and people eventually moved on. Brandon's post office finally closed in 1963. A few stoic citizens and some abandoned buildings still remain.

BRANDON HOTEL: The Brandon Hotel was built sometime before 1911.

Situated on a corner in town, the Brandon Hotel was owned and operated by State Representative Cline, circa 1911–12.

KIT CARSON COUNTY

Founded in 1889, the county was named for the famous scout Kit Carson. Its county seat is Burlington. The county is not without surprises. In 1928, Denver's well-known amusement park Elitch Gardens sold its old, broken-down carousel, produced in Philadelphia in 1905, to Kit Carson County for the princely sum of $1,250 and laughed.

The carousel had lost favor with big city patrons because its animals were stationary and did not move up and down, even though it revolved faster than most merry-go-rounds (twelve miles per hour, one and a half times the average speed). This historic carousel is the sixth of seventy-four produced by the Philadelphia Toboggan Company between 1904 and 1933.

Unfortunate county officials lost their reelection bids over this "reckless" decision to purchase a merry-go-round in hard economic times. Yet time would vindicate them, and Kit Carson County has had the last laugh.

The carousel's murals, horses, chariots, outer rim and Wurlitzer Monster Military Band organ have been restored to original mint condition. The revitalized relic made its debut at the county fairgrounds in Burlington as the Kit Carson County Carousel. In 1987, the carousel was designated a National Historic Landmark and is still open to the public. It is considered a priceless treasure.

Seibert

The small stagecoach stop of Hoyt, between the Republican River and Buffalo Creek, was once located four miles north of the present town of Seibert. When the railroad came through Colorado in 1888, Seibert was founded and named after railroad official Henry Seibert. As businesses began moving into Seibert, Hoyt was reduced to a virtual ghost town and assimilated into the new railroad town.

AUNT KATE HOTEL: Built in 1899 by Bert Hendricks, this hotel's lumber was hauled by wagon from Hieghler, Nebraska. The hotel was torn down in 1935 for the first post office. It was operated by "Aunt" Kate Hutchins.

Aunt Kate Hotel, July 4, 1908, showing "Aunt" Kate Hutchins (right foreground) in a white dress, marked by an "X."

Lincoln County

Lincoln County was established in 1889 and named for President Abraham Lincoln, with Hugo as its county seat. The Union Pacific Railway was constructed soon after. A second railroad, the Rock Island, was built across northern Lincoln County, crossing the Union Pacific at Limon. The Rock Island declared bankruptcy nearly a century after it arrived; its tracks from Limon west to Colorado Springs were dismantled, and its right of way was used in places for walking and bike paths.

Arriba

Arriba was founded on controversy. In 1888, Charles A. Creel set up a real estate business on the present town site and had a specific vision in mind for his community. The Rock Island Railroad track was laid nearby, and for several years, Arriba grew according to Creel's plan.

That is, until C.C. Coleman purchased land adjacent to Arriba in 1904. By 1907, he was selling lots for a new town, Frontier City. Creel had refused

The Hotel Colorado in Arriba, circa 1919.

to sell property to anyone planning to build saloons, but the cagey Coleman allowed one to be built on one of his lots, close to Creel's home. Thus, the "wets" and the "drys" squared off, Creel shouldering a personal obligation to protect his people of Arriba from the evils of "demon drink."

Creel marked off a parcel of land a half block wide and three blocks long between Arriba and Frontier City. Called "Devil's Lane" and "Hell's Half-Acre," the strip would soon become "No Man's Land." But thirsty Arribans gladly faced the perils of No Man's Land to get to that jazzy new saloon.

Creel took more drastic measures, digging a ditch the length of the strip, eight feet wide by eight feet deep. But a court order, obtained by one of his fellow citizens, required Creel to fill in his ditch. So Creel hired one Will Emerson to construct a barbed-wire fence along the strip. Emerson was kept busy during the day replacing the fence, which was repeatedly taken down at night by unknown revelers.

With Creel's death in 1918, the feud abated. Creel's widow, who didn't have her whole heart in the controversy, donated a parcel of No Man's Land for a church and then sold off the rest of the lots. Frontier City was soon absorbed by Arriba and included in the town's charter. The Frontier City saloon is gone, but Creel's house remains, keeping sullen vigil across No Man's Land, now identified only by the town's east–west streets changing names when they cross the former hostile line of demarcation.

HOTEL COLORADO: The Hotel Colorado was built sometime before 1919.

Hugo

This town was named for Hugo Richards, a railroad official later influential in California financial circles. The town boasts the Hugo Municipal Pool, a Works Progress Administration (WPA) project. Labor on it was halted twice, once for the WPA crew to finish the Hugo gymnasium and again in 1937 for the crew to spread poison bait in the battle against grasshoppers. Walls of the pool's bathhouse are adobe, a mixing of traditional construction techniques with modern design.

Hugo's 1909 roundhouse, associated with the operation of the Union Pacific Railroad in eastern Colorado, is the state's most intact Union Pacific example, one of only four surviving roundhouses in Colorado.

GRAYMONT HOTEL: This hotel was built before 1911.

PROWERS COUNTY

This county was created from Bent County in 1889 and named for John W. Prowers, pioneer and cattleman. It includes both sides of the Arkansas River for thirty-nine miles west from the Colorado-Kansas state line.

Lamar

In 1866, well-to-do cattleman A.R. Black was asked by railroad "town site platters" to donate land from his original settlement of Blackwell. Black refused, even though he was warned that another town would start up next to his if he declined the offer. Before long, another landowner complied and sold property to the railroad promoters. In no time, the Blackwell depot was moved three miles west, and its sign was changed to Lamar, named for Lucius Q. Lamar, secretary of the interior under President Cleveland. People flocked in, enticed by the idea of free land. Lamar was the last town to be established in this dubious fashion and is the youngest significant town on the main line of the Santa Fe Railway. Located on the Arkansas River in southeastern Colorado, Lamar is the Prowers County seat, with agriculture as its main industry.

HOTEL BEN-MAR: This hotel was built sometime before 1909 and was later renamed Maxwell House. From 1909 to 1911, the Hotel Ben-Mar was

A postcard of the Hotel Ben-Mar, circa 1929.

The newly constructed Davies Hotel, 1902.

operated by retired doctor Lillian Heath Nelson and her husband, Louis J. Nelson. Nelson was a former member of President McKinley's honor guard, and Heath, a pioneer in her field, was the first woman to practice medicine in Wyoming. As a teen in the 1880s, she assisted Dr. Thomas Maghee, a Union Pacific Railroad physician, when she was obliged to disguise herself in young man's clothing for her safety. Heath was a graduate of the College of Physicians and Surgeons in Keokuk, Iowa.

The hotel was given a makeover and became known as Maxwell House in the 1930s. Still later, it became the Stockman's Bar and Inn. The historic Hotel Ben-Mar is still standing, but its latest facelift is a modernized front façade to disguise it as a store.

DAVIES HOTEL/PAYNE HOTEL: The Davies Hotel was built in 1902 at 122 North Main Street. It is still standing. The Davies' location near the railroad depot ensured it a steady stream of lodgers. Builders utilized locally quarried sandstone for the outer walls, and the hotel is now on the National Register of Historic Places.

WASHINGTON COUNTY

Most of the Native American population was forced out of eastern Colorado and moved onto reservations by 1870. In 1885, the Union Pacific Railroad constructed a branch line from Julesburg to Denver. With the government willing to provide up to 480 acres of cheap land to each family and the railroads actively promoting the area by reducing transportation rates on special "immigrant cars," the population boomed. Missing from the promotional advertising for "cheap land" was any mention of disgruntled Native Americans yet residing in the area.

That same year, the president ordered that all illegal fences be removed from public lands so farmers and ranchers would perceive an equal footing.

The county was named in honor of President George Washington.

Akron

Akron was built along the Burlington Northern Railroad line in the northeastern plains. It was once the only established town along the line, holding much importance during the railroad era. Named for Akron, Ohio, Akron is the Washington County seat, fifty miles west of Denver.

HOTEL AKRON: This hotel was built circa 1886.

A postcard of the Hotel Akron, promoting the area to prospective new residents. It reads: "We are enjoying ourselves at the Hotel Akron...Located on the great Burlington Route. The only commercially pure Fullers Earth in America is found here. The oil and gas wells discovered are second to none. The gold placer grounds, none richer. The best farm lands in the United States, with room for 1,000,000 people. Come, help develop this productive part of Colorado, and secure for yourself and your family a home, where health and riches can be found."

YUMA COUNTY

Named for the Yuma tribe, this county was created in 1889 from part of Washington County. Yuma's southern half was added in 1903 from Arapahoe County. Yuma County has one geographic distinction. Where the Arikaree River flows out of Yuma County into Cheyenne County, Kansas, at 3,315 feet in elevation, the lowest point in Colorado, this crossing point is on record as the highest low point of any U.S. state.

Yuma

The town of Yuma was incorporated in 1887. Each September, Yuma celebrates its farming history during Old Threshers Day. This small community in northeast Colorado grows more corn than any county in the state.

LEFT HOTEL: Built prior to 1916, the Left Hotel was destroyed by a tornado in 1916. Nothing left.

Northeast Central Counties

While enterprising ranchers opened their properties to guests, people with extra bedrooms spiffed them up to rent for income. This was particularly true of single women. The boldest might even put up a sign proclaiming her home a hotel. In going over a record of forgotten lodgings from more than a century ago, it becomes plain that such practice was often as much the rule as the exception.

Millionaires like Spencer Penrose and F.O. Stanley built fabulous resort hotels—the BROADMOOR and the Stanley—still thriving today. By stark contrast, there was the Timberline Hotel of Holy Cross City and the California Hotel of Independence (both ghost towns today), which operated simultaneously to a clientele in stark contrast to the prosperous resort trade.

Arapahoe County

Arapahoe County calls itself "Colorado's First County" for gold discovered in 1858—one year before the Pikes Peak gold rush—along the South Platte River in present-day Englewood. Arapahoe originally stretched from present-day Sheridan Boulevard 160 miles east to the Kansas border. Its county seat is Littleton. Today, Arapahoe County is part of the Denver-Aurora Metropolitan Area.

Deer Trail

This town was founded as a Kansas Pacific Railway station in 1870 and soon became a shipping point for grain, livestock and eggs. By the late 1920s, Deer Trail supported two banks, five grocery stores and three hotels. Deer Trail sits quietly on the eastern plains and is the Home of the World's First Rodeo.

OASIS HOTEL: Built prior to 1911, the Oasis was a two-story, stone corner building.

Denver

(Spans three counties: Arapahoe, Boulder and Denver.) Called the "Mile-High City," Denver's elevation is 5,280 feet above sea level. Denver City was founded in 1858 as a mining town during the Pikes Peak gold rush. General William Larimer, a land speculator from Kansas, staked a claim on the bluff overlooking the confluence of the South Platte River and Cherry Creek and named the town for Kansas territorial governor James W. Denver, who never bothered to visit his namesake.

In 1867, Denver City became the Colorado Territorial Capital and shortened its name. In 1876, Colorado was admitted to the Union.

HOTEL ABBOT: Located at Nineteenth and Curtis Streets, the Hotel Abbot was operated by O.E. Taussig in 1904.

ADAMS HOTEL: Located at Eighteenth and Welton Streets from 1902 to 1969, this hotel was designed by Harold W. and Vigio Baerresen (Baerresen Brothers Architectural firm) of Denver. The interior was designed by Gilbert Charles Jaka and featured a copper dome twenty-five feet above the dining/ballroom floor, a push-button elevator and a phone in every room. It was operated by W.F. Sperry in 1904. The hotel closed in 1969 and was razed for a parking lot.

ALAMO HOTEL: Located on Seventeenth Street, the Alamo Hotel was advertised on 1910 postcards as "only three blocks from UNION DEPOT."

ALBANY HOTEL: Built prior to 1893 at Seventeenth and Stout Streets, the Albany Hotel was remodeled in 1893. It was managed by W. Maher Hotel Co. in 1904 and was demolished in 1977.

HOTEL ALBERT: Built in 1900 at Seventeenth and Welton Streets, the Hotel Albert was operated by F.A. Oppenheim in 1904.

ALDINE HOTEL: Built before 1904 at Seventeenth and Ogden Streets, the Aldine Hotel was operated by Mrs. A.M. Brewster in 1904.

ALVORD HOUSE: Built in the 1870s at Eighteenth and Larimer Streets, the Alvord House was a three-story brick hotel with a flat roof. Its long porch wrapped around the front corner and served as a two-story gallery.

AMERICAN HOUSE: Built before 1904 at Sixteenth and Blake Streets, the American House was operated by C.H. Smith in 1904.

ARLINGTON HOUSE: Built before 1904 at 1520–36 Sixteenth Street, the Arlington House was operated by A.E. Keables in 1904.

DENVER AUDITORIUM HOTEL: This hotel was located at Fourteenth and Stout Streets.

HOTEL AYRES: Listed in the 1916 city directory at 1441 Logan Street, Denver, the former address of the Hotel Ayers is now a parking lot.

THE BATIONE (later called the Granite Hotel): This hotel was built prior to 1900 at 1720 Larimer Street.

THE BELVOIR: Located at 737 East Sixteenth Street, the Belvoir was a family hotel operated by Mrs. C.J. Apple in 1904.

THE BINFORD HOTEL: This hotel was built sometime before 1892.

HOTEL BROADWAY: Built before 1899 at 1539 Broadway, the Hotel Broadway was operated by A.H. Green in 1904.

BROADWELL HOTEL: This hotel was built before June 1860 at the corner of Larimer and Sixteenth Streets.

*THE BROWN PALACE: 321 Seventeenth Street, Denver, CO 80202; 303-297-3111; brownpalace.com.

In 1888, businessman Henry Cordes Brown (no relation to Unsinkable Molly) purchased several acres, including a triangular plot at the corner of Broadway, Tremont and Seventeenth Streets, where he initially grazed his cow. The Windsor Hotel, then one of Denver's most prestigious hotels, had offended Brown by refusing him entrance because he was wearing cowboy attire. In retaliation, Brown decided to build a hotel that would put the Windsor to shame.

In 1888, he retained architect Frank E. Edbrooke to design a hotel, the likes of which had never been seen—an "unprecedented hotel" in the Richardsonian Romanesque style. Four years and $1.6 million later, the Brown Palace opened. Its exterior was red Colorado granite and Arizona sandstone, with an Italian Renaissance lobby, composed of marble and Mexican onyx, rising to an eight-story atrium leading the eye to a stained-glass ceiling.

More than seven hundred wrought-iron grillwork panels circle the lobby from the second through the seventh floors. Two panels are upside down. It has been theorized that this may be to exemplify the imperfection of man, who must always put a flaw in his handiwork. Or possibly the misplaced panels were slipped in by a disgruntled workman.

The hotel's triangular shape allows sunlight to illuminate each of its almost three hundred rooms, and Rocky Mountain spring water still flows to every room from its original 720-foot-deep artesian well. Bottled well water is also available to hotel guests. A huge carousel oven, more than sixty years old and one of only three known, still turns out melba toast, macaroons and other baked goods daily.

In 1911, the hotel saw a scandalous murder, which has been recorded in recent years in the book *Murder at the Brown Palace*. The lurid tale involves an unsympathetic heroine, a four-way romance, an inept gunman and the death of both an innocent bystander and one contender for the dubious female. Apparently, even elegant surroundings cannot stem the tide of unbridled passion.

But history favors the Brown Palace. Beginning in 1905, every president since Theodore Roosevelt has visited the hotel, except the unadventurous Calvin Coolidge. Eisenhower stayed there so frequently that the hotel was often referred to as the western White House.

The Brown Palace is known for its elegant teas, served in the onyx lobby. However, ladies in hats, gloves and finery who come to tea at the end of January are treated to much more than little cakes and dainty sandwiches. Every year since 1945, next to the tea area, the lobby also displays the annual Stock Show championship steer, which enters on a red carpet and drinks from a silver bowl. This gracious fifteen-hundred- to two-thousand-pound guest, resplendent in mascara and a wreath, seems to have no beef about sharing public honors

A postcard of the onyx lobby. Interior of the Brown Palace Hotel, circa 1900.

with the less celebrated ladies at their tea. No doubt, Henry Brown and his cow appreciate the spectacle.

So it seems Brown has had the last laugh. While the Windsor went on to inglorious ruin and was razed in the 1950s, the Brown Palace has never once closed its doors since opening well over a century ago. Today, it remains what it was originally meant to be—a magnificent, unprecedented hotel.

CHEESMAN HOTEL: This hotel was built sometime before 1904 at Broadway and Seventeenth Streets.

COLUMBIA HOTEL: Built in 1878 as a retail building at 1330 Seventeenth (at Market) Street, the Columbia was converted into a hotel in 1892 by Frank Goodnow. It was operated by J.B. Laughlin in 1904 and managed by Walter J. Neville in 1909. The hotel was known for its ninety guest rooms with hot running water. It was a convenient stop thanks to its proximity to Union Station. Still operating as a hotel in the 1960s, today the building is used for retail and office space and is known as the Market Center.

HOTEL COSMOPOLITAN: Opened in June 1926 (originally as the Hotel Metropole) at 1760 Broadway, in 1884, the Cosmopolitan was demolished in a controlled explosion.

HOTEL CREST: Opened in July 1910, the Hotel Crest was a "Flatiron" building located at Welton, Broadway and Twentieth Avenues. The hotel's large electric sign rose from the rooftop, and businesses filled its first floor.

THE DEVONSHIRE: Located at 1425 Logan Street, the Devonshire was a family hotel operated by Mrs. W.R. Jones in 1904.

DODGE HOTEL: Built sometime before 1904 at Broadway near Eighteenth Street, the Dodge Hotel was operated by E.R. Cooper in 1904.

DOVER HOTEL: Built sometime before 1913 at 1744 Glenarm Place, the hotel's postcard from about 1930 gives its rates as one dollar and up, offers eighty rooms, and lists the owner as Sam Sclavenitis.

DREXEL HOTEL: This hotel was built about 1907 on Seventeenth Street.

ELEVENTH AVENUE HOTEL: Located on Eleventh Avenue, C.W. Adams was the proprietor of this hotel. A 1911 postcard claims, "High class family hotel, modern throughout."

THE ELMORE: Located at 1320 Stout Street, the Elmore was operated by C.W. Williams in 1904.

THE ERHARD HOTEL: This hotel was built sometime before 1922.

FRONTIER HOTEL: This hotel was located on Fourteenth Street.

GEM HOTEL: Located at 1746 Curtis Street, the Gem Hotel was a three-story building with a stone front and an attached theater.

GRAND CENTRAL HOTEL: Built before 1904 at Seventeenth and Wazee Streets, the Grand Central was operated by H.A. Beard in 1904.

GRANITE HOTEL: Built before 1889 at the Corner of Larimer and Fifteenth Streets, the Granite Hotel was a four-story, gray granite, stained-glass building, the brainchild of W.M. and G.W. Clayton. It was designed by John Roberts as a department store. It housed an upscale retail business operated by M.J. McNamara, but the location turned out to be below expectations. In 1889, McNamara moved his trade to Sixteenth and California Streets. A few years later, his new store became the Denver Dry Goods Company.

The original stone store became known as the Granite Building, and in 1906, it was renamed the Granite Rooms. It passed through several owners, becoming the Granite Hotel somewhere along the way. The development of Denver's Larimer Square in the 1970s brought an unexpected boom to the Granite; its highly visible, prime location made it a significant fixture in the downtown renewal project.

THE GRAYMONT: Built before 1904 at Eighteenth and California Streets, the Graymont was operated by J.M. Bent in 1904.

HOTEL GREAT NORTHERN: This hotel was located at 1612 Larimer Street.

GUARDS HALL: This hotel was built in 1873 and razed in 1915.

INTER-OCEAN HOTEL: Opened in October 1873 at the corner of Sixteenth and Blake Streets, the Inter-Ocean Hotel was built by Barney L. Ford, a prominent African American businessman and former slave who became a politically influential millionaire.

Ford escaped slavery in South Carolina via the Underground Railroad and went west, where he tried his luck at prospecting and struck it rich. He opened a barbershop in Denver, but the fire of 1863 destroyed much of the town, including his shop. Ford, an innate businessman, took out a $9,000 loan and built the successful People's Restaurant, still standing at 1514 Blake Street. From the profits of this business, he built and ran the elegant Inter-Ocean Hotel in town. After this success, Ford built a second Inter-Ocean Hotel in Cheyenne, Wyoming, which stressed his finances considerably. In 1882, he built a house in Breckenridge at 111 East Washington Avenue, designed for him, his wife, Julia, and their children by prominent craftsman Elias Nashold. The house still stands, and is known as the Barney Ford House Museum. Ford also opened Ford's Restaurant and Chop House in Breckenridge.

Until his death in 1902, Ford was active in supporting African American rights, literacy classes and education for freed people of color in Colorado. A stained-glass window in the Colorado Statehouse commemorates Ford, the early civil rights pioneer, who worked tirelessly to elevate Denver's African American community.

Barney Ford's Inter-Ocean Hotel, circa 1900.

In 1904, the Inter-Ocean Hotel was managed by G.N. Stein. Unfortunately for history, the building was razed in the early 1970s.

KOPPER'S HOTEL: Located at 1215–19 Twentieth Street, Kopper's Hotel was operated by Albert Kopper in 1904.

LAFAYETTE HOTEL: Located at 1576 Lincoln Street, the Lafayette Hotel was a family hotel operated by J.B. Penton. The 1904–05 directory lists the Kassler House at Sixteenth and Lincoln. Number 1576 Lincoln Street is listed as the Lafayette Hotel. The hotel is not listed before 1900.

LEADVILLE HOUSE: The hotel was located on Blake Street (see Revere Hotel).

LINDELL HOTEL: Built before 1904 at Eleventh and Larimer Streets, the Lindell Hotel was operated by Erhard Menig in 1904.

MARTINEZ HOTEL: Built before 1904 at 3463 Blake Street, the Martinez Hotel was operated by the Martinez brothers in 1904.

METROPOLITAN HOTEL: Built sometime before 1904 at Nineteenth and Market Streets, the Metropolitan was operated by Hans Bollen in 1904.

HOTEL METROPOLE: Built in 1889 at Eighteenth and Broadway, the Hotel Metropole was operated by Otto Kappler and later became the Cosmopolitan Hotel, from 1926 to 1984 (see Cosmopolitan Hotel).

HOTEL MIDLAND: This hotel was built about 1908 at the corner of Seventeenth and Arapahoe Streets.

NATIONAL HOTEL: This hotel was located at 1713 Larimer Street.

NEW MARKHAM HOTEL: Built before 1904 at Seventeenth and Lawrence Streets, the New Markham Hotel was operated by Hughes & Nolan in 1904.

NEW UNION HOTEL: Built before 1904 at Seventeenth and Blake Streets, the New Union was operated by W.A. Arey in 1904.

OCCIDENTAL HOTEL: Built before 1904 at 1640 Blake Street, the Occidental Hotel was operated by C.C. Johnson in 1904.

*OXFORD HOTEL: 303-628-5400, 800-228-5838; theoxfordhotel.com.

Built in 1891 at Seventeenth and Wazee Sreets, the Oxford Hotel was located across from Union Station. The Oxford is Denver's oldest existing historic hotel, constructed in 1891. Colorado's leading architect, Frank E. Edbrooke, designed the five-story brick hotel one year before designing the Brown Palace. Edbrooke's Oxford met Denver's need for a "really first-class hotel" near Union Depot. Edbrooke, a Union soldier during the Civil War, was to become recognized as one of Denver's most significant architects. He designed such local landmarks as the Tabor Block and the Grand Opera House, the State Capitol Building, Loretto Heights Academy, the Masonic Temple, the Chamber of Commerce Building, the Denver Dry Goods Company and the Colorado State Museum.

Edbrooke's innovative Oxford had its own power plant, steam heat system, electric and gas lighting and separate water closets in its bathrooms. Dining tables held cut glassware, Haviland china and silverware inscribed with "Oxford." The hotel's novelty, the "vertical railway," or elevator, carried guests to the upper stories. The Oxford survived the Silver Panic of 1893, and while banks, railroads and mines collapsed, the Oxford prospered.

The Oxford is home to McCormick's Fish House, specializing in fresh seafood. It also houses the sophisticated Art Deco Cruise Room, both of which opened the day following the repeal of Prohibition. The first keg of locally brewed Coors beer was served in the Cruise Room lounge.

Among the Oxford's more recent contributions to Denver's streetscape is the installation of a replica of its original entrance canopy. Both the handsome welcoming awning, which had been removed in the 1930s, and its detailed, scrolled iron framework were designed and constructed by local artisans.

Since 1991, the hotel has carried on a tradition begun by the Denver Dry Goods Company decades earlier: the annual Holiday Dolls' Tea Party, in which local girls bring their best doll and their mother. Reporter Frances Melrose, who recalled these teas from her childhood, suggested that the

Oxford host the event. While the moms enjoy tea at grown-up tables, children and dolls sip cocoa and cider at child-sized tables with pink tablecloths.

The Oxford offers eighty guest rooms and is also a repository of an extensive collection by western artists such as Frederick Remington, portrait painter Herndon Davis and French master Bougereau. Century-old scenic stained glass may be viewed in McCormick's Restaurant, and etched Art Deco panels in the Cruise Room add more grace and interest. The Oxford, full of wonderful surprises, is listed on the National Registry of Historic Places.

Now in its 112th year, the timeless Oxford still welcomes guests, serving Denver's downtown with the same elegance ascribed to its long-standing history.

PARK HOTEL: Built sometime before 1904 at 1717 Eighteenth Street, the Park Hotel was operated by L.P. Dixon in 1904.

THE PIERCE HOTEL: Built before 1904 at the corner of California and Thirteenth Streets, the Pierce Hotel's advertising postcard states, "Three minutes from the heart of town."

HOTEL PLAZA: This hotel was built sometime before 1905 at 330 Fifteenth Street, at the corner of Tremont.

PLYMOUTH PLACE HOTEL (later Cory Hotel): Built in 1898 at 1560–72 Broadway, Plymouth Place was owned by George W. Kassler and operated by Mrs. J.B. Edwards in 1904.

The Oxford Hotel boasts its newly restored canopy. Union Depot is in the background. *Photo courtesy of the Oxford Hotel.*

The Kassler Block was built as offices and rental rooms by local architects Marean and Norton. Its most remarkable feature was a ballroom for society affairs, fitted with parlors and dressing rooms and decorated in Moorish style with ornamental electric ceiling lights. A gallery with Moorish arches led to the ballroom, trimmed in woodwork of white enamel. It was intended for exclusive use of the Capital Hill 400, and while it did host numerous events, in 1906 "Kassler Hall" was removed from the building, likely due to insufficient bookings. Later, the building again underwent remodeling.

REVERE HOTEL: Built sometime before 1898 at 1421–27 Blake Street, next to the Leadville Hotel, the Revere was operated by J. and W.H. Graves in 1904.

ST. ELMO HOTEL: Built before 1904 at Seventeenth and Blake Streets, the St. Elmo Hotel was operated by F.W. O'Neill in 1904.

ST. FRANCIS HOTEL: This hotel was built sometime before 1904 at Fourteenth and Tremont Streets.

ST. JAMES HOTEL: Built between 1900 and 1920 on Curtis Street, near Sixteenth Street, the St. James Hotel was operated by H.H. Blake in 1904. Signs for the hotel read: "Baths available in basement" and "Furnished rooms for transients." It was torn down in 1920 for construction of a theater.

The St. James Hotel, circa 1905.

St. Nicholas Hotel: This hotel was built before 1904 at Stout and Eighteenth Streets.

The Shirley: Located at Seventeenth and Broadway, the Shirley was built in 1902 by Colonel Dodge and was operated by E.R. Cooper in 1904. The Shirley was very elegant; it had its own farm and dairy for serving fresh products. The hotel was back to back with the Savoy Hotel, both facing Seventeenth Street, with the Shirley at Lincoln and the Savoy at Broadway. The two consolidated in 1921, becoming the Shirley-Savoy Hotel, and operating as one until the early 1960s, when the Shirley building was razed. The Savoy section continued to operate until it was razed in early 1970.

*The Standish Hotel: Built before 1909 across from the Denver Dry Goods Company at 1530 California Street in Denver, the Standish is still in operation (303-534-3231).

Sylvania Hotel: Built before 1914 at 1331 Court Place, the Sylvania Hotel was operating in 1918.

Union Stock Yards Hotel: Built before 1904 at the Union Stock Yards, this hotel was operated by M. Owen in 1904.

The Vallejo: Located at 1420 Logan Avenue, the Vallejo was a family hotel built before 1904, operated by J.E. Birkenmaier.

Hotel Victor: Built before 1904 at Sixteenth and Larimer Streets, the Victor was operated by C.H. Stubbs in 1904.

The Waddell: Built before 1904 at West Thirty-second Avenue and Bert Street, operated by J.N. McDonald in 1904.

Ward's Hotel: Built before 1904 at Cline Street and Fisk Avenue, Ward's Hotel was operated by E.F. Ward in 1904.

Western Hotel: Built before 1904 at Twelfth and Larimer Streets, the Western was operated by C. Schneider in 1904.

Windsor Hotel: Opened on June 12, 1880, and closed in 1958, the Windsor was razed in 1959. It was located at Eighteenth and Larimer Streets, built by an English firm under the direction of James Duff.

The hotel, designed by W. Boyington of Chicago, was intended to represent the glamour and refinement of England's Windsor Castle and occupied nine city lots. Its exterior featured sandstone from Fort Collins, gray stone from near Castle Rock, striped awnings above first-floor windows and a large American flag flown from its prominent corner tower. There were separate ladies' and gentlemen's entrances, with iron porte-cochères and a marble floored lobby. Fine cuisine was served on Haviland china, and the hotel's mahogany bar was inlaid with silver dollars.

The hotel is often associated with one of its owners, silver king H.A.W. Tabor, and his mistress, "Baby" Doe, whom he married following his divorce. They maintained the Windsor's bridal suite, after spending their wedding night there. Its rooms were decorated with gold silk brocade and costly walnut furnishings, to which, with typical extravagance, Tabor added a gold-plated bathtub and doorknobs.

The beautiful (Elizabeth McCourt) Baby Doe Tabor (1854–1935) honored Tabor's dying wishes after he lost his fortune when silver crashed. She tenaciously held onto his Leadville silver mine, the Matchless, until she was found frozen to death in its cabin. Both are buried in the Tabor plot at Mount Olivet Cemetery in Denver.

Among the roster of the Windsor's elite guests were literary giants Rudyard Kipling, Mark Twain, Robert Louis Stevenson, Oscar Wilde and George Bernard Shaw, as well as Presidents Cleveland, Grant, the ubiquitous Teddy Roosevelt and the three-hundred-pound Taft, who got stuck in Baby Doe's bathtub and required bellhops to extricate him. (She had since moved on.)

The Windsor's front stairs were called the "suicide staircase," for the many who leapt to their deaths down it, after losing their fortunes in one of the upstairs gambling rooms. A light behind a stair post supposedly cast the shadow of a devil's head.

A postcard of the Windsor Hotel, Denver, circa 1900.

By 1917, Denver's lively downtown had moved away from the Windsor, leaving the once grand hotel to slide into gradual ruin. Heroic efforts were made in the 1930s to revive it, and artist Herndon Davis painted murals on its bar with portraits of famous former guests. These murals are now in the collection of the Oxford Hotel. Unfortunately, by the 1950s, the aging hotel had become a notorious landmark on skid row, opening its once refined rooms to transients and alcoholics, taunted as "the flophouse with marble fireplaces." By 1958, it had closed and auctioned off its elegant furnishings. The Windsor Hotel was torn down one year later.

Littleton (Includes Morrison)

Littleton dates to the 1859 Pikes Peak gold rush, which lured not only miners but also merchants and farmers to the community. Richard Sullivan Little, a New Hampshire engineer, went west to work on irrigation systems, settled in present-day Littleton and brought out his wife in 1862. The Littles and their neighbors built the Rough and Ready Flour Mill in 1867, providing the community with a sound economic base. The town was incorporated in 1890.

*CLIFF HOUSE HOTEL: 121 Stone Street, Morrison, CO 80465; 303-697-9732; cliffhouselodge.net.

This hotel was built in 1874 by George Morrison, founder of the town of Morrison. The prominent stone building was built on a rise and had a clipped, cross-gabled roof. It was also known as Evergreen House and was later called Swiss Cottage.

In 1895, George Morrison's home became the Cliff House Hotel and still stands as one of the oldest remaining structures in Morrison. It is now a bed-and-breakfast, with eight themed private cottages surrounding the mansion. Part of the main house serves as a lobby, and its great room is the setting for special events. The National Register of Historic Places selected most of the town of Morrison as a historic district, which includes the Cliff House.

Through the years, the Cliff House has gone through several incarnations, from private home to inn and back again. Known today as the Cliff House Lodge, the property has been fully restored and once more resumes its role as gracious host to visiting guests.

COMMERCIAL HOTEL: This hotel was operated by H.G. Smith in 1904.

COTTAGE GROVE HOTEL: This hotel was operated by W.R. Collins in 1904.

LITTLETON HOTEL: This hotel was operated by A.N. Abbott in 1904.

Above: The historic Cliff House Lodge in Morrison. *Photo courtesy of the Cliff House Lodge.*

Below: A postcard of the veranda at John Brisben Walker's Mount Morrison Hotel, circa 1912.

MOUNT MORRISON HOTEL AND CASINO: Built in 1874, this hotel was demolished in 1982.

John Brisben Walker, owner of *Cosmopolitan* magazine, sold his publication to William Randolph Hearst and moved to Colorado. In 1908, Walker purchased property owned by Sacred Heart College that included a large portion of Red Rocks. He reworked the old college building into a Casino Resort for Governor John Evans.

Walker's son, John B. Walker Jr., ran the Casino and became Morrison's third mayor in 1909. But misfortune beset Walker Sr.'s empire, and most of his holdings were sold in the 1920s. The hotel became known as Hillcrest Inn in the 1930s. In 1943, it was a retreat for the Poor Sisters of St. Francis and was last known as Pine Haven. After a long period of decline, it was razed in 1982.

Walker is remembered locally for his commitment to preserving the natural beauty and parks of Jefferson County. The view from his hotel was described in Walker's promotional brochure of 1909 as follows: "The distant mountain top…the first view you get of the Mount Morrison railway (Mount Morrison Incline) as you sit on the broad veranda of the Mount Morrison Hotel and look upon the lavish splashes of color with which nature has painted the scenery of one of the most beautiful realistic art settings in the world."

BOULDER COUNTY

Boulder is one of seventeen counties created by the Territory of Colorado in 1861. The county was named for Boulder Creek, so called for the abundance of, what else, boulders in the area.

Boulder

Arapahoe Indians traditionally wintered at the base of the foothills in the area until the town of Boulder, once part of Nebraska Territory, was founded in 1859. In 1873, the railroad was extended to Boulder, and three years later, Colorado was granted statehood. In 1875, the first cornerstone was laid for the first building of the state university, and Colorado University officially opened in Boulder on September 5, 1877.

ALBANY HOTEL: By 1916, the Albany Hotel had become the YMCA.
BOULDER HOUSE: This hotel was built before 1875–80 at Eleventh and Pearl Streets.

*HOTEL BOULDERADO: 2115 Thirteenth Street, Boulder, CO 80302; 303-442-4344, 866-539-0036; boulderado.com.

This hotel was designed by William Redding and Son. Boulder depended on tourism but had no first-class hotel. By 1906, a subscription drive had raised enough money to start construction on one, and the Hotel Boulderado opened for business on New Year's Day 1909. Its name was suggested by William Rathvon, who incorporated the words "Boulder" and "Colorado" so guests would remember where they had stayed. The structure employed sandstone from the former Colorado Red Sandstone Company of Fort Collins. The Boulderado has restored its famous stained-glass canopy ceiling and retained its original cantilevered cherry staircase, extending from the basement up to the fifth floor.

William Beattie was hotel manager until 1917, when he placed the hotel's operations in the hands of Hugh Mark. Mark and his family lived in the hotel until he passed away in 1937. Mark, a beloved figure in town, had done much to promote the Boulderado, advertising it outside of the state and encouraging people to visit Boulder. The hotel, as practical as it is grand, appeals to both the visitor of average income and the wealthy, and has hosted many University of Colorado guests, among them Robert Frost.

The hotel hosts Q's Restaurant and the Corner Bar. Q's specializes in seasonal, local, organic ingredients and offers an outstanding wine list. Q's is a "green" establishment, practicing responsible recycling and composting, and making use of eco-friendly products.

A postcard of the Hotel Boulderado, circa 1912.

THE BOWEN: This hotel was built sometime before 1904.

THE COLORADO HOTEL: This hotel was built sometime before 1904.

GERMAN HOUSE: This hotel was built sometime before 1904.

LITTLE HOTEL: This hotel was built sometime before 1904.

THE O'CONNOR: Built in 1875 at 1302 Walnut Street, this hotel went by the name The O'Connor until 1917. The building continued to operate as a hotel under various names until 1955.

ST. JULIAN HOTEL: This hotel was built sometime before 1904.

El Dora Lake

El Dora Lake is located in the Roosevelt National Forest. The mining town of Eldora, once expected to rival Cripple Creek, foundered shortly after its 1898 silver boom. Today, it is a quiet community, and the nearest town is Nederland.

PINE LOG INN: Built by 1912, the Pine Log Inn was advertised as a family fishing resort within sixty miles of Denver.

El Dorado Springs

The town was named for the legendary city of gold. By 1910, Eldorado Springs was known for its Big Radium Pool, then reported to be the largest swimming pool in the United States, and was called the Coney Island of the West. The town is located at the mouth of Eldorado Canyon on South Boulder Creek.

A lively carnival atmosphere prevailed at El Dorado; many people came to watch renowned daredevil Ivy Baldwin (forerunner of stunt man types like Evel Knievel) cross the canyon on a tightrope suspended 582 feet off the ground. Others entertained themselves at dancing pavilions or with games on the midway, roller-skating or fishing.

It was still a booming resort until the 1938 flood destroyed the dance hall and all but removed the swimming pool. Flooding is still a concern along the creek, but the historic pool fed from the artesian spring remains open and has been a popular resort since it first opened in 1905.

*EL DORADO SPRINGS: This is now known as Eldorado Springs Pool at 294 Artesian Drive (303-499-9640).

ELDORADO HOTEL: In 1908, the grand Eldorado Hotel opened, with the finest room in the house costing $2.50 per night. The hotel was perched above one of the swimming pools and a dance hall, and offered forty rooms.

Lyons

Located at the confluence of the North and South St. Vrain Creeks, the area was settled by farmers and cattle ranchers in the 1850s and 1860s. Lyons was founded in 1880 by Edward S. Lyon, who began quarrying red sandstone outcroppings in the region. This local sandstone is considered the hardest in the world, having a unique red to salmon color. Lyon was one of the first to establish the quarry trade in town, but others followed. The railroad's arrival in the 1890s gave the quarries a significant boost, but in 1910–12, the cement industry killed the sandstone industry, and rock production stopped. The only sandstone construction during this time was the new University of Colorado campus.

BILLINGS RANCH: This guest ranch was operated by Mrs. H.C. Billings in 1904.
COPELAND'S RANCH (Allen's Park): This guest ranch was operated by J.B. Copeland in 1904.
ELKHORN RANCH: This guest ranch hotel was operated by A.C. Fisher in 1904.
LYONS HOUSE: This hotel was operated by Mrs. A. Halliday in 1904.
ST. VRAIN HOTEL: Built before 1872 on the 300 block of Main Street, this hotel burned down in the 1879 fire but was apparently rebuilt. It was operated by W.P. Flanders in 1904.
STEAMBOAT VILLA: This hotel was operated by James Lowe in 1904.
WELCH'S RESORT: This hotel was operated by W.A. Welch in 1904.

Nederland

This town began as a trading post between Utes and Europeans during the 1850s. Its first economic boom came when silver ore was discovered in 1859, followed by the discovery of gold and tungsten. The town has been through three different mining booms and busts for these metals.

Originally called Brownsville after a miner named Brown, Nederland was also called Layton and Middle Boulder before taking its present name in 1873, credited to Dutch mining investors who purchased the Caribou Mill.

Nederland is also the site of an unusual carousel. In 1910, carousel maker Charles Looff of Denmark delivered one of his creations to Saltair Park, outside Salt Lake City, Utah. It survived a fire and a windstorm, which blew the roller coaster onto the carousel, requiring it to be rebuilt with only two rows of animals from its original four. In 1986, when the carousel was sold to a buyer who only wanted its animals, Scott Harrison of Nederland bought

First Antlers Hotel, circa 1890s. The hotel was operated by Charles Huggins in 1904. In 1907, Mrs. Roose opened her new Antlers Hotel in town.

the empty frame and brought it to town. Over the next twenty-two years, he and friends restored the frame and carved a menagerie of thirty-eight wooden animals to complete it. The Carousel of Happiness is now a result of new and old creation, the spirit of the century-old carousel waiting for adults to revisit their youth and the young to enjoy a spin. E-mail info@ carouselofhappiness.org for more information.

ANTLERS HOTEL: This hotel was built in the 1870s for Abel Goss by Erasmus Parsons. In the 1890s, Mrs. Roose opened it as a small tourist hotel, maintaining it until about 1907, when she built a larger hotel at Nederland. The Hetzer family occupied the place for several years.

BROWN'S MOUNTAIN HOUSE: This hotel was built about the 1860s by Nathan Bolly Brown. Nederland was first called Brownsville and Brown's Crossing because of this building, thought to be first in the area.

HETZER HOTEL (also known as McKenzie House): Built in 1877, this hotel burned down in 1939. It was owned by J.D. McKenzie at the time. It was a well-known lodging place in the region.

Wall Street: Ghost Town

Established about 1899, Wall Street is now an abandoned mining community, fenced off from the public.

WALL STREET HOTEL: Built before 1904, the Wall Street Hotel was operated by Mrs. D. Blanchard in 1904.

Ward

Ward, located on a mountainside at the top of Left Hand Canyon, thirty-six miles northwest of Denver, is a former mining settlement founded in 1860, following discovery of gold at nearby Gold Hill. It was one of the richest towns in the state during the Colorado Gold Rush and was named for Calvin Ward, who struck it rich on the site known as Miser's Dream. In 1901, forty-five of Ward's buildings were destroyed by a fire that started in the Hotel McClancy, though the mines' wealth led to immediate rebuilding. The town was largely deserted by the 1920s, but construction of the Peak-to-Peak Highway in the 1930s fueled its revival.

Hotel McClancy, 1893.

COLUMBIA HOTEL: Built before 1904, the Columbia was operated by Mrs. M.S. Buck in 1904 and was owned by Albert L. and Emma Hauburg Fairhurst. In 1919, Emma Fairhurst was written up in the *Hotel Monthly* for the Columbia's unique fireplace, which she built using ore specimens collected from various mines in Ward. The hotel is now a private residence.

C&N HOTEL: Built before 1904, the C&N was operated by Mrs. M.F. Thompson.

HOTEL McCLANCY: Built before 1899, the Hotel McClancy burned down in 1901 when its stove caught fire and took most of the town with it. The hotel was rebuilt soon after the fire.

CLEAR CREEK COUNTY

Clear Creek is one of seventeen original counties created in 1861 and one of only two to have its original boundaries. It was named for Clear Creek, which runs from the continental divide through the county.

Empire

This town was founded in 1860 by miners who believed the promise of gold and silver in the area would one day make their town as great as New York, the Empire State.

The Peck House: over a century of welcome and as inviting as ever. *Courtesy of the Peck House.*

*The Peck House: 83 Sunny Avenue, Empire, CO; 303-569-9870.

The Peck House Hotel and Restaurant was built in 1862. From 1858 to 1865, many settlers arrived to stake a claim in Empire, among them James Peck and his three sons, who settled here in 1860 and built a house. In 1862, Mary Grace Parsons Peck brought the family goods by oxcart and joined her family. Due to the area's increase of newly arriving residents, Mrs. Peck soon found herself a full-time innkeeper.

Notables, including P.T. Barnum, Ulysses S. Grant and General Sherman, have stayed at the Peck House. The Peck family owned the hotel until the death of James Peck's grandson, Howard, in the 1940s. Present owners Gary and Sally St. Clair first visited the Peck House on their honeymoon, and by March 1981, they had arranged to purchase the hotel.

The Peck House is the oldest continually operating hotel in Colorado. Many of the antiques throughout the hotel came by oxcart with the Peck family in 1862.

Georgetown

Georgetown is 8,530 feet above sea level. Once a rough-and-tumble town founded during the Pikes Peak gold rush of 1859 by two Kentucky prospectors, George and David Griffith, Georgetown (named for the older brother) has acquired grace with age. While the town expanded following the discovery of silver, it was never a true mining town but rather a trade center for surrounding camps.

In 1868, the Georgetown area had a problem. It was rich in minerals, but getting the ore out of the mountains posed a challenge. This was solved in 1877, when Jay Gould brought the Colorado Central Railroad to Georgetown and Silver Plume, and the ores were then easily taken to Denver for smelting.

The arrival of the narrow gauge railway increased the town's prosperity. A portion of the original route has been restored between Georgetown and Silver Plume and is now a tourist train called the Georgetown Loop.

With its well-preserved, historic Victorian buildings and lively character, Georgetown is today an inviting village, not to be missed.

Eldridge Hotel: This hotel was built before 1880 on Rose Street.
Elliot House Hotel: This hotel was built sometime before 1897.
Ennis Hotel: This hotel was built sometime before 1897.
Grand Central Hotel: Built sometime between the 1870s and 1890s, the Grand Central is a two-story, four-square frame building.

July 5, 1897, Georgetown. A parade in front of the Elliot House Hotel.

HOTEL DE PARIS: Begun about 1878 at Sixth and Griffith Streets, this hotel was constructed from three separate older buildings by the eccentric Louis Dupuy, owner and proprietor, and was completed in 1890. The building has a stucco finish and is painted with French and American flags.

The mysterious story of Louis Dupuy, of Alencon, France, and his unlikely hotel is fascinating. The hotel-museum documents the lives of Dupuy, his housekeeper, Sophie Galley, and two later proprietors.

Born Adolphe Francois Gerard in 1844, by 1869, he had arrived in Denver under the new name of Louis Dupuy. In 1873, Dupuy was injured in a mine blast while rescuing a co-worker. Injuries ended his brief mining days, and he was required to seek other work. Georgetown citizens, knowing of his heroism, took up a collection to help him purchase a local bakery in 1875. By 1878, he had expanded it into the Hotel de Paris and installed the widowed Sophie Galley as his housekeeper. By 1890, Dupuy had enlarged his hotel to the size it is today.

Dupuy installed electricity, and added the bronze statue of Justice on the roof. Even though rough-hewn miners formed a portion of his clientele, Dupuy did not skimp on the quality of his French cuisine or his rooms.

The dining room floor featured alternating boards of light and dark walnut and maple, supporting a fountain filled with fresh trout. Elegance was

The Hotel de Paris is now operated as a museum by the National Society of the Colonial Dames of America in the state of Colorado.

Dupuy's byword, and he furnished his hotel with fine linens, silver, French wine and Haviland china. Running water was installed, with marble sinks.

Dupuy, consummate chef and businessman, was also thought to be something of a misogynist, often turning away potential female guests when he had vacancies. However, he and the faithful Sophie Galley, an older, illiterate Frenchwoman, were close companions. In 1900, Dupuy died of pneumonia, leaving the hotel to Galley, who only lived a few years after inheriting it. She and Dupuy are buried next to each other in Georgetown's cemetery.

In a twist of irony, the hotel established by the man who distrusted most women is now owned by an entire organization of them. After changing hands twice, following Galley's death, the hotel was acquired in 1954 by the National Society of Colonial Dames of America, which now operates it as the Hotel de Paris Museum (303-569-2311).

YATES HOUSE HOTEL: This hotel was built sometime before 1880 on Rose Street.

Graymont

This small settlement was at one time the western end of the line for the Colorado Central Railroad, which ran from Georgetown to Graymont. The line was built by the Georgetown, Breckenridge and Leadville Railroad.

JENNINGS HOTEL: This hotel was built sometime before 1884.

Idaho Springs

Local legend says that the town was named for annual visits to the area's radium hot springs made by a Native American chief and his tribe, who reportedly came from Idaho to bathe in the healing waters.

Idaho Springs began as a gold rush town in 1859, when George Jackson found gold at the confluence of the Chicago and Clear Creeks. As word of his discovery spread, hopeful fortune-seekers flocked in, establishing a settlement. Further mining development expanded the town, and as Idaho Springs grew, so did the need for housing.

Dumont's Boarding House, aka German House, was owned by the Dumont family in 1901. "German House" and "Office" were printed on the first-floor windows. The "X" indicates a Dumont child. The man marked by a "D," in a hat and suspenders in the doorway, is the proprietor.

In 1860, the significance of its hot springs brought about the building of Ocean Bath and Mammoth Bath, which began to draw tourists. Idaho Springs was soon marketed as the "Saratoga of the Rocky Mountains." Enterprising innkeepers recognized opportunity and built their hostelries, and civilization came to yet another raggedy mining town.

BEEBEE HOUSE HOTEL: 1600 Colorado Blvd., Idaho Springs, CO. Built before 1870, the Beebee House was a one-hundred-room mountain hotel; its dining room was run by Mrs. Beebee. President Grant stayed here in 1873. The hotel was razed in 1907, and Elks Lodge #607 was built on the site.

CLUB HOTEL: Built before 1904, the Club Hotel was operated by E.W. Dillon in 1904.

COLORADO HOTEL: No information available.

DUMONT'S BOARDING HOUSE/GERMAN HOUSE: This hotel was built sometime before 1901.

*ECHO LAKE LODGE: Built in 1926, Echo Lake Lodge is no longer a hotel. At a 10,600-foot elevation, it is now a tourist gift shop and restaurant. It is located a few miles from Idaho Springs on State Highway 103, at the junction of Mt. Evans Road. The restaurant specializes in home-baked pies (303-567-2138).

HANSON'S LODGE: Built about 1883 at 1601 Colorado Boulevard, Hanson's is one of the area's oldest hotels, once known as the Wright Hotel. President Teddy Roosevelt and Doc Holliday stayed here (but not at the same time). The building was logged over in 1922. Hanson's Lodge currently operates as a hostel with nineteen rentable rooms and is for sale. The rustic hotel is on the State and National Historic Registers.

*HOT SPRINGS HOTEL/RADIUM HOT SPRINGS HOTEL: 302 Soda Creek Road, Idaho Springs, CO 80452; 303-989-6666; indianhotsprings.com.

In 1863, Dr. E.S. Cummings purchased the springs, built a bathhouse and operated a middling business on the property. He sold to Harrison Montague, who improved bathing facilities and built a hotel. Montague sold his profitable business to investors, who constructed a much larger and finer hotel around Montague's original. The Hot Springs Hotel and its reputed healing waters continued to draw continuous clientele until World War II, when business declined for a time before picking up again.

The springs and their historic lodge are still open, known today as Indian Hot Springs. They offer massage, spa treatments and overnight accommodations.

PORTLAND HOTEL: Built before 1904, the Portland Hotel was operated by George Pierce in 1904.

TROCADERO HOTEL: Built sometime before 1908, the rustic, three-gabled hotel was operating in 1908.

Silver Plume

Silver Plume is a former silver mining camp along Clear Creek whose fortunes rose and fell with the gold rush, the silver boom and the silver panic.

LA VETA: Built before 1904, La Veta was operated by Mrs. E. Rowe in 1904.
NEW WINDSOR HOTEL: Built before 1892, the New Windsor was operated by Mrs. H.F. Lampshire in 1904.

DOUGLAS COUNTY

Douglas is one of the original seventeen counties created in the Colorado Territory in 1861, named in honor of U.S. senator Stephen A. Douglas of Illinois. The county seat became Castle Rock in 1874.

Decker Springs

Decker Springs was a medicinal springs and fishing resort, fifteen miles by stage (costing seventy-five cents each way) from South Platte Station. It was owned by Maurice Weinberger about 1900 and reached via the Colorado and Southern Railway.

DECKER'S: Built before 1904, this hotel was operated by S.D. Decker.

Larkspur

This small community is located eleven miles south of Castle Rock.

CLOVER HILL RANCH: This hotel was operated by Mrs. Dakan in 1904.
NOE HOTEL: This hotel was operated by J.R. Noe in 1904.
NANCHANT INN: This hotel was operated by C.H. Underwood in 1904.
PERRY PARK RANCH: Built about 1880s, this hotel burned down.
   In 1870, John D. Perry, president of the Kansas Pacific Railroad, purchased four thousand acres, eventually named Perry Park. In 1888, Perry and his investors attempted to turn the property into a resort. A dam was built on

Bear Creek, creating Lake Wauconda, and a large hotel was built south of the lake. But attempts to extend the railroad through Larkspur into the park failed, and the resort did not prosper. The ranch changed hands many times until the mid-1900s. The hotel was eventually destroyed by fire.

GILPIN COUNTY

Gilpin County was formed in 1861. In 1859, John H. Gregory staked the first mining claim in what would soon become known as the "Richest Square Mile on Earth." The spot, marked by the Gregory Monument, is near the city limits of Central City and Black Hawk. By mid-1859, more than twenty-five thousand people lived in and around Gregory Gulch, in unimaginably squalid conditions.

Black Hawk

Black Hawk was named for a local milling company, which had taken the name of a Native American chief. Founded in 1859 during the Pikes Peak gold rush adjacent to Central City, Black Hawk flourished in the late 1800s due to construction of mills and a rail link to Golden. It declined during the 1900s but has revived considerably following the legalization of casino gambling. In 2010, the Black Hawk city council passed a controversial law banning the riding of bicycles in the town, so peddlers beware.

THE GILPIN HOTEL: 111 Main Street, Black Hawk, CO 80422; 303-582-1133. This hotel was built before 1896. The three-story brick hotel had a porch with a second-floor gallery, and in 1905, a sign over its main door read, "The Gilpin Hotel, J. Klein, Prop." No longer a hotel, the Gilpin is now a casino.

Central City

With John Gregory's discovery of the "Gregory Lode" in 1859 near Central City, 8,496 feet above sea level, the gold rush was on. Central City's population rose to ten thousand, all seeking fortune. Things got testy. In 1861, the town recorded 217 fistfights, 97 gunfights, 11 knife fights and 1 dogfight. Amazingly, no one was killed. A fire in 1874 razed most of the frame-constructed town, which was rebuilt of brick and stone and is mostly still standing.

Interior lobby of the Teller House.

EUREKA HOUSE: This hotel was built before 1897 on Eureka Street.

TELLER HOUSE: 120 Eureka Street, Central City, CO 80422.

Construction on the hotel was begun in 1871. When a local subscription drive to build the hotel fell short, Henry M. Teller, Colorado Central Railroad president, provided most of the funds to complete the project. It was stated that Teller House was the finest hotel west of the Mississippi River, named for its greatest benefactor, who was also one of Colorado's first senators.

The hotel was furnished in style and offered an excellent billiard room and a bar with murals by English artist Charles Stanley, supposedly painted for his hotel bill. The Teller House acquired its most famous work of art following a 1930s renovation, in which artist Herndon Davis painted a life-size portrait of his wife on the saloon floor, titled *The Face on the Barroom Floor* after a well-known Victorian poem.

Among the hotel's famous visitors was President Ulysses Grant, who, prior to arrival, was supposedly asked by the hotel for a plaster mold of his hindquarters so a chamber pot of appropriate dimensions could be installed in his room. It is not known whether Grant complied with the request. Bathrooms had not yet been installed in the Teller.

The Teller House was owned by the Teller family for several generations but survived in the later twentieth century primarily as a tourist attraction. No longer an operating hotel, the Teller House is now a casino.

Rollinsville

This town was named for Joseph Rollins, a surveyor with the railroads, about 1880.

HOTEL ROLLINSVILLE: This hotel was built about 1915–20.

Tolland (Formerly Mammoth)

Tolland, originally called Mammoth, was an early mining town and stage stop on the line across Rollins Pass. In 1904, the Toll family, significant area landholders, changed the town's name to Tolland—if one has influence, such things are possible. They built the Toll Inn, and Mrs. Toll was postmistress of the town. But following completion of the Moffatt Tunnel, Tolland's business declined, and the train passed without stopping. Today, Tolland is a quiet community, mostly of summer homes. Many original buildings survive and have been restored.

TOLL INN: Built sometime between 1904 and 1925, the Toll Inn was owned and operated by Mrs. Charles Toll, who built the hotel with twenty-six rooms for railroad passengers. It was a popular stop for one-day excursions from Denver, offering a restaurant, lunch stand, post office, souvenir store and picnic pavilion.

JEFFERSON COUNTY

Located along the Front Range of the Rockies, Jefferson County is part of the Denver metropolitan area. Organized in 1861, Jefferson County was named for Thomas Jefferson.

Buffalo Creek

Buffalo Creek was established about 1877 along the stream of the same name, and Buffalo Creek Post Office opened in 1878. The town has more than once been destroyed by fire.

HOTEL HUDSON: This hotel was built sometime before 1910.

Deansbury/Strontia Springs

Located in Platte Canyon, this town was a medicinal spring.

STRONTIA SPRINGS HOTEL: This hotel was built about 1884 as a summer resort located beside the South Platte River on the Denver, South Park and Pacific line of the Colorado and Southern Railroad. The hotel was a brick structure, with a large native stone fireplace. It was operated by the Strontia Springs Hotel Co. in 1904, and later burned down.

Deansbury Lodge and the two-story Strontia Springs Hotel. Its balcony and gazebo are labeled, "Strontia Medicinal Water."

Evergreen

In 1859, Thomas Bergen established a ranch and stage stop north of present-day Evergreen. In 1875, homesteader Dwight P. Wilmot was credited for naming the area "Evergreen." The town's economy thrived due to the canyon's thick forest and Denver's demand for lumber. By the 1880s,

Evergreen had six operating sawmills. Road improvements through Bear Creek Canyon in 1911 drew tourists and helped it become a well-known resort destination.

ARTIST'S VIEW: Built before 1904, Artist's View was operated by J. Murphy in 1904.

BABCOCK INN: Built before 1904, the Babcock Inn was operated by J.D. Babcock in 1904.

*BROOK FOREST INN: 8136 Brook Forest Road, Evergreen, CO 80439; 303-679-1521, 866-679-1521.

From a deserted cabin purchased in 1913, which was renovated and expanded by Edwin Welz of Vienna and his wife, Riggi, of Switzerland, the Brook Forest Inn became one of the area's most attractive lodges. It opened in 1919. The mountains reminded the Welz family of the Alps. Welz was postmaster in 1921 for Brook Forest, and the inn served as the region's post office until 1931.

The original cabin, built by a family named Westerfield, is now the lobby and pub. In 1927, the dining room was added to the main building, with two stories above it.

In 1937, a medieval turret of white and rose quartz was completed across the street and is known as the "Bell Tower House." The Welz family operated the inn until 1946, when it was sold, changing hands several times over the years.

The historic Brook Forest Inn.

The historic Brook Forest Inn has been host to the elite, such as President Theodore Roosevelt, Liberace and the Unsinkable Molly Brown. The inn also hosts fables of secret subversive gatherings decades ago and gold hidden in its walls. Paranormal ghost tales of a stable hand and a chambermaid further color its lore.

Today, the handsome historic inn and restaurant are open and welcoming guests.

EVERGREEN HOTEL: This hotel was built about 1900.

GREYSTONE GUEST RANCH: Built in 1916 in the English Tudor style, this ranch was opened periodically to the public. Notables Cornelia Otis Skinner, Groucho Marx, rocket scientist Werner Von Braun and Mae West stayed on the property. Now a private residence, it sits four and a half miles west of Evergreen Lake at a seventy-five-hundred-foot elevation, with views of Mount Evans.

HINES HOTEL: Built sometime before 1904, the Hines was operated by J.J. Hines in 1904.

A traveler's luggage sticker from Troutdale-in-the-Pines.

STRONGHURST INN: This hotel was built sometime before 1915.

TROUTDALE HOTEL/TROUTDALE-IN-THE-PINES: This hotel was built in the 1890s. The resort began as a cluster of cabins and a single-story hotel, operated in 1904 by the Troutdale Hotel Co. In 1920, Harry Sidles, a Nebraska businessman, expanded it into an elegant hotel with a pond, pool and golf course. Until the late 1930s, Troutdale thrived as one of the Rockies' most popular resorts. But World War II and hard times forced it to close, and despite efforts to resurrect the resort, it was razed in 1994.

*CAMP NEOSHO: Built about the 1890s, Camp Neosho was operated by Wheelock & Mackey in 1904. This twenty-five-room log lodge, listed on the National Register of Historic Places, was owned by only two families before Jefferson County bought the property in 1974.

In the 1890s, Mary Neosho Williams, a Civil War widow, and her daughter, Josepha, were among wealthy Denverites who camped at Evergreen. They acquired a simple log structure and hired Jock Spence, a Scottish carpenter, to convert it into a summer cottage. The property was named Camp Neosho for Mrs. Williams's middle name. Overnight guests stayed in tents with wood floors, stoves and double canvas walls. It later became the retreat of Dr. Josepha Williams, one of the first female doctors in Colorado. In 1889, she operated a sanitarium in Denver for patients suffering from tubercular and lung diseases. Camp Neosho, operated by the Jefferson County Historical Society, is now the Hiwan Homestead Museum in Evergreen (4208 South Timbervale Drive, Evergreen, CO 80439; 720-497-7650).

Golden

Golden, established during the gold rush of 1859, is a former mining camp first called Golden City for Thomas L. Golden. Situated along Clear Creek, Golden is home to the Colorado School of Mines, the National Renewable Energy Laboratory, the National Earthquake Information Center and Coors Brewing Company.

ALVORD HOUSE: This hotel was built before 1873 on Thirteenth Street.

ASTOR HOUSE HOTEL: This hotel was built in 1867 by Seth Lake. It was constructed of local hand-cut stone and operated as a boarding and rooming house until 1971. It replaced an earlier frame hotel that Lake had built, which he called Lake House, and was the town's first stone building, with walls eighteen inches thick. The hotel changed hands repeatedly and was known chronologically as the Castle Rock House and Boston House, until it

Alvord House, Golden.

was saved from demolition and designated a historic landmark. It became a museum in 1973, operated by the Golden History Museums (303-278-3557, goldenhistorymuseums.org/astorhousemuseum).

AVENUE HOTEL: Built before 1873 on Washington Avenue, this hotel was operated by Lake and Wells in 1904.

HOTEL BELLA VISTA (originally the St. Bernard): This hotel was built in 1881 on Ford Street by Nicholls and Canmann, architects. It was a three-story, massive brick edifice with hip roof, a square domed tower, fourteen fireplace chimneys and an iron front façade. It was torn down in 1920.

BURGESS HOUSE HOTEL: This hotel was built before 1866 as the Burgess Block by Thomas W. Burgess, at 1015 Ford Street.

CRAWFORD HOUSE: Built before 1904, the Crawford House was operated by John McEchron in 1904.

GOLDEN HOUSE HOTEL: Built before 1878, the Golden House Hotel was destroyed by fire in 1878.

OVERLAND HOTEL: This hotel was built before 1908 at Twelfth and Washington Avenues.

Pine Grove

Pine Grove, established in 1886, has many historic homes and shops. Located in the foothills southwest of Denver, Pine Grove is a quaint mountain community.

ELK CANYON HOTEL: Built before 1904, the Elk Canyon Hotel was operated by W.E. Burr in 1904.

Wellington Lake

This was a favorite fishing and camping location, approximately ten miles from Bailey, Colorado.

WELLINGTON HOTEL: Built before 1904, the Wellington was operated by J.P.C. Dickinson in 1904.

LARIMER COUNTY

Larimer County sits at the edge of the Eastern Plains, along the border of Wyoming. The county was named for the founder of Denver, William Larimer Jr., who is thought to never have set foot in it. Though it is one of Colorado's original seventeen counties, mining did not play a large role in area history. The settlement of Larimer County was based almost entirely on agriculture, specifically dry land farming, a technique successfully employed for generations by western Native Americans.

Cache le Poudre River

The river, west of Fort Collins, was reportedly named by early French explorers, who hid their gunpowder beside its banks. This area remains unspoiled, offering opportunity for whitewater kayaking and rafting, with trails for biking and hiking.

CAMPTON'S RESORT: This hotel was built sometime before 1906.

Drake

Drake is a small community in Big Thompson Canyon, with its post office near the Rocky Mountain National Park.

*Forks Hotel: 1597 West Highway 34, Drake, CO 80515; 970-669-2380; http://www.riverforksinn.com/index.html.

Built in 1875, the Forks Hotel is now known as the Historic River Forks Inn. A century ago, the hotel was reached via the Loveland to Estes Park Auto Road. It is now accessible by paved Highway 34. The inn, situated on twenty-three acres, has been run by various people over the years, including Enos Mills, "Father of the Rocky Mountain National Park," who leased the lodge for two years about 1912. The Forks is still in operation as a bed-and-breakfast and is famous for its fly-fishing.

Two Stanley Steamers beside the Forks Hotel, 1909. It was an early stage and mail stop.

Estes Park

This area was named for miner Joel Estes, a Kentuckian who struck it rich in California and discovered the Estes Valley in 1859. A year later, he moved his wife and thirteen children, along with a herd of cattle, to a meadow in the valley, where they lived until 1866.

In 1864, William Byers, owner and editor of the *Rocky Mountain News*, named the area Estes Park in honor of Estes. But Estes found cattle ranching difficult in the high altitude and short growing season, and he sold his homestead to Griff Evans, who turned it into a dude ranch. One of Evans's European guests, the Earl of Dunraven, so admired the area that he decided to buy the entire valley for his personal hunting preserve. Fortunately, his intentions were thwarted by area residents and mountain men.

In 1903, F.O. Stanley, co-inventor of the Stanley Steamer automobile with his twin brother, F.E. Stanley, came from Massachusetts seeking a cure for tuberculosis. The climate was so beneficial to his health that he settled in Estes Park and built the Stanley Hotel, which opened in 1909, costing more than half a million dollars.

*BALD PATE INN: 4900 South Highway 7, Estes Park, CO 80517; 970-586-6151.

Built in 1917 by the Mace family, the inn is now a bed-and-breakfast and restaurant. The inn's sign, a ring of seven keys, hangs on the front entrance. It was named after a popular mystery novel, *The Seven Keys to Bald Pate*, by Lord Earl Derr Biggers.

In keeping with the novel's story line, the Mace family gave each visitor to the inn his or her very own key. This tradition continued until World War II, when metal became so expensive that the innkeepers were no longer able to give keys away. Loyal guests were so disappointed that they began their own tradition of bringing a key back to the inn each year. Thus began the world's largest key collection, which boasts over twenty thousand keys.

In 1986, the Smith family purchased the property. Only the second family to own and operate the inn, for the past twenty-five years they have welcomed guests to experience the enchantment of Bald Pate Inn.

*HOTEL CRAGS: 300 Riverside Drive, Estes Park, CO 80517; 970-586-6066, 800-521-3131 (reservations); cragslodge.com.

This hotel first opened in 1914 and is the third-oldest lodge in Estes Park. The historic Crags Lodge was built by Enoch "Joe" Mills, author, photographer, lecturer, English professor and football coach at the University of Colorado. He was also the brother of Enos Mills, who helped established the Rocky Mountain National Park.

Born in 1880, Joe Mills made his first trip to Estes Park alone, at the age of sixteen. He recorded his first response to the Estes Valley: "Before me loomed the Rockies, strangely unreal in the moonlight and yet very like the mountains of my imagination. I gazed spellbound. My dream was realized."

Joe and his wife, Ethel, built their dream lodge on the north shoulder of Prospect Mountain, naming it Crags Lodge for the rocks that form the mountainside. Many famous people, including Robert Frost, have found their stay at Crags Lodge inspiring.

Mills originally furnished the hotel with rustic pieces from the Old Hickory Furniture Company. Through the years, much of the original furniture was removed, but present managers have remodeled and decorated the rooms with similar Old Hickory furnishings and period-inspired pieces. Some of Mills's original tables and chairs, purchased in 1914, can be found in the lodge's restaurant, the View, which overlooks the town of Estes Park. The restaurant is open for dinner from mid-May to mid-October.

The Crags Lodge is today the main building of the Golden Eagle Resort and is listed on the National Register of Historic Places.

*ELKHORN LODGE: 600 West Elkhorn Avenue, Estes Park, CO 80517; 970-586-4416; elkhornlodge.org.

The James family's guest ranch venture began in 1874, when they discovered that taking in lodgers, elk hunting and bringing the meat to Denver were more lucrative careers than cattle ranching. But this popular practice, ongoing from the 1870s until 1900, seriously reduced the elk population. So in 1913, the Elkhorn and other forward-thinking ranches, using forty specially built wagons, began transporting elk back into Estes Park to rebuild the diminishing herds.

Guests would once order fresh trout for meals from nearby Fall River. But as the trout population declined, the Elkhorn began the state's second fish hatchery in the 1890s. After the State of Colorado moved the hatchery, it became, and is now, the Elkhorn's private trout pond.

The Elkhorn operated the area's first icehouse. Blocks of ice from Fall River were cut in winter, transported by horse and wagon and stored in the icehouse for refrigerating foods.

The Elkhorn's Main Lodge was built in 1871 and has two large fireplaces. The James family purchased Stickley furniture for the lobby, and some of the finest Stickley pieces known still remain at the Elkhorn. Stickley investors are frequently sent to view the Elkhorn's collection, and the Stickley Museum has offered to purchase some of its furnishings.

As the Elkhorn expanded, it constructed new, and incorporated existing, buildings. Among the buildings upgraded for use is the Coach House, the original stagecoach terminal. In 1877, a four-dollar ticket would purchase a one-way trip from Lyons to Estes Park.

The rustic ranch offers stables and riding trails, camping, swimming, hiking and "no license required" trout fishing, with equipment provided.

The Elkhorn is the oldest guest ranch still operating in the Rockies, two blocks from downtown Estes Park—an authentic piece of Colorado history listed on the National Register of Historic Places.

ESTES PARK HOTEL: Built before 1904, the Estes Park Hotel was operated by C.E. Lester and Co. in 1904.

FALL RIVER LODGE: This hotel was built in 1915 on the south side of Fall River Road by Dan and Minnie March. The handsome Arts and Crafts resort was a compound of a main lodge, fourteen cabins and a corral. But to enforce its policy of keeping the land unspoiled, the National Park Service bought the property in 1959 from J. Russell McKelvey and, sadly, in 1960 removed all evidence of the lodge and its outbuildings, restoring the property to its original state.

By 1904, the former James Ranch in Estes Park had become the Elkhorn Lodge. Photo circa 1900.

The Horseshoe Inn, circa 1910.

HIGHLAND HOTEL: Built before 1904, the Highland was operated by H.W. Ferguson in 1904.

HORSESHOE INN: Built sometime between 1908 and 1931 by Willard Ashton, the Horseshoe Inn was intentionally razed by fire in 1931. The Arts and Crafts–style Horseshoe was the first casualty of the National Park's policy against building on park property, and many private lodges were removed. Just what standards determined who was forced to remove and who permitted to remain is not entirely clear.

THE LEWISTON: The Lewiston was advertised in the 1920s as Estes Park's "premier hotel."

LONG'S PEAK INN: Built in 1902, Long's Peak Inn was originally owned by Reverend Elkanah Lamb. It was then purchased and run by his cousin, Enos Mills, a naturalist. Operating in 1904, it burned down and was rebuilt in 1906. It burned down again in 1949.

Born in 1870 in Kansas, Enos A. Mills was a sickly child. His parents, hoping his health would improve, sent him at age fourteen to stay in Estes Park. He worked briefly at the Elkhorn Lodge, before arriving at the ranch of his cousins, Reverend and Mrs. Elkanah Lamb. Their son, Carlyle, took Mills on his first climb up Long's Peak, which inspired him to become a mountain guide. Mills spent time wandering the area, picking a spot across

Mrs. Enos Mills meets with Tennessee naturalist Robert Sparks Walker near her cabin to discuss her late husband's work, 1950.

from the Lambs' ranch to build a cabin, which he finished in two summers. It is today the Enos Mills Cabin Museum.

Mills met great naturalist John Muir in 1889, on a trip to San Francisco. The two established a friendship. Muir had an enormous impact on Mills, influencing his philosophy and future life.

In 1901, Mills bought the Lamb Ranch. In 1904, he changed its name to Long's Peak Inn. He took people on nature walks and up Long's Peak, which he climbed to the summit more than one hundred times. He preferred small groups, especially children who were open to his teachings. Mills sought to draw guests' attention to the natural world. From the foot of Long's Peak, he did not want them distracted by city life and did not permit smoking, drinking, card playing or music in the lobby. But he respected any activity in guest rooms as private business. Adventurous guests flocked in, in greater numbers each year.

In the spring of 1906, the inn's main building burned down. Mills was on a lecture tour but hurried back to begin rebuilding without blueprints or drawings. The main lodge and its cabins were reconstructed from deadfall timber gathered from an old forest fire. The kitchen and dining room were able to serve guests by July that same year.

Mills's writing and speaking engagements began to take more time, and he also began training more nature guides for his Trail School. He emphasized not only nomenclature but also every aspect of nature and its constant changes, even along familiar paths. Mills's methods of nature guiding would become the standard for field interpretation in the National Park Service.

But Mills did not disapprove of comforts such as steam heat, electricity, plumbing, feather beds and flannel sheets. Long's Peak Inn had three telephones. At one time, the famous radio announcer Lowell Thomas declared that the three best restaurants in Colorado were at the Brown Palace, the BROADMOOR Hotel and Long's Peak Inn.

Long's Peak Inn, circa 1911–20.

Mills kept journals and began lecturing in 1891, a practice he continued until his death. Guests awaited his evening talks at the inn by campfire or by the lobby fireplace at day's end. His writing career finally flourished, and he wrote his adventures and observations in a clear, poetic manner that engaged rather than bored readers. National magazines published his articles; he later put them into book form. In 1909, his first major book, *Wild Life of the Rockies*, brought national attention. His second, *The Spell of the Rockies*, was his bestseller. In all, Mills wrote over eighteen nonfiction books.

Mills died suddenly at the age of fifty-two in 1922 from an abscessed tooth. His wife, Esther, sold Long's Peak Inn in 1946. In 1949, the main lodge burned again, and ownership changed hands a number of times over the years.

Mills is considered the "Father of Rocky Mountain National Park," which was established in 1915.

THE RUSTIC HOTEL: Built before 1904, the Rustic Hotel was operated by the Rustic Hotel Co. in 1904.

STEAD'S HOTEL/SPRAGUE HOTEL: This was a rustic resort built by Abner E. Sprague in Moraine Park about 1900 and operated by Sprague & Stead. Sprague sold it to his nephew, J.D. "Jim" Stead, about 1904.

*THE STANLEY HOTEL: 333 Wonderview Avenue, Estes Park, CO 80517; 970-586-3371, 800-976-1377; www.stanleyhotel.com.

In 1903, F.O. Stanley, inventor of the Stanley Steamer automobile, came to Estes Park for his health. Impressed by the beauty of the valley and grateful for his improvement, he decided to invest his money and future there.

In 1909, he opened the elegant, Georgian-style Stanley Hotel, nestled against the Rockies, seventy-five hundred feet above sea level. The Stanley

The elegant Stanley Hotel.

is reportedly haunted. Its founders, F.O. and Flora Stanley, are said to be some of its ghostly guests. Mr. Stanley plays piano in the music room and also shows up in the billiard room and lobby. A visit to the Stanley inspired author Stephen King to write *The Shining*.

The hotel hosts Steamers Café and Cascades Restaurant, with a wide variety of offerings, including buffalo, trout and lamb. The glamorous hotel is listed on the National Register of Historic Places.

TIMBERLINE HOTEL: Built about 1900, the Timberline is a tiny rustic shack. Its postcard claims, "One of many well-known in the park, situated on Long's Peak Trail, 11,000 feet elevation."

WIND RIVER LODGE: Built before 1904, the Wind River Lodge was operated by Guy La Coste in 1904.

Fort Collins

In 1849, a party of Cherokee Indians passed through Larimer County en route to California; their path was later identified as the Cherokee Trail. In 1862, discovery of gold in Idaho drew many prospectors away from Colorado, the most direct route to Idaho being the Cherokee Trail, blazed thirteen years earlier.

In the 1860s and '70s, open-range cattle ranching and an increasing number of small farms dominated Larimer County. The Colorado Central Railroad arrived in the 1870s, and in 1903, the Great Western sugar beet processing plant was built. The climate and plentiful grazing were found to support sheep, and many fruit orchards, particularly cherry, were planted.

In 1862, Camp Collins, named for Colonel William Collins, commander of the Eleventh Ohio Cavalry in Fort Laramie, Wyoming, was established on the Cache La Poudre River, a stopover for those traveling the Overland Trail. In 1869, the settlement was a town, incorporated as Fort Collins. Fort Collins is home of Colorado State University.

AUNTIE STANES MESS HALL AND HOTEL: This hotel was builte about 1870.

BATTERSON HOUSE: Built before 1904, this hotel was operated by William Batterson in 1904.

CHEROKEE PARK HOTEL: Built before 1904, this hotel was operated by William Compton in 1904.

COMMERCIAL HOTEL: Built of brick sometime before 1904 at 172 North College Avenue, the Commercial Hotel was operated by D.N. Harris in 1904. An earlier wooden hotel, the Agricultural Hotel, once occupied this site. After renovations, the Commercial became the Northern Hotel in 1905.

FORKS HOTEL: Built before 1904, the Forks was operated by W.O. Mossman in 1904. It was notable for piles of antlers flanking both sides of the entry.

Auntie Stanes Mess Hall and Hotel, the first dwelling house in Fort Collins.

KEYSTONE HOTEL: Built before 1900 on the Cache la Poudre River, the Keystone was operated by J. Zimmerman in 1904. Its postcards advertised "all the comfort of a home. Music ball and billiard halls. Fine trout fishing, nice drives, boating, shooting, inspiring scenery."

LARIMER HOUSE: Built before 1904, the Larimer House was operated by F. Gowder in 1904.

LINDEN HOTEL: Built in 1882–83 by Abner Loomis and Charles Andrews at 250 Walnut Street, the Linden was a corner brick building, constructed as the Poudre Valley Bank, which simultaneously also housed other businesses. From 1917 to 1983, the Linden Hotel occupied the building. It was operated by J.A. Davidson in 1904.

LIVERMORE HOUSE: Built before 1904, the Livermore House was operated by C.W. Ramer in 1904.

NORTHERN HOTEL: Located at 172 North College Avenue, in 1905, major renovation completely altered the Commercial Hotel when a stained-glass dome was added in the dining room and the name was changed to the Northern Hotel. A fourth floor was added in 1924 and an Art Deco façade in the 1930s. Most recently, the Northern has reopened as affordable senior housing.

POUDRE VALLEY HOTEL: Built before 1904, this hotel was operated by L.P. Wasson in 1904.

RUSTIC HOUSE: Built before 1904, this hotel was operated by W.J. Steele in 1904.

TEDMON HOUSE: Built before 1904, this hotel was operated by H.M. Sholine in 1904.

Loveland

Loveland was founded in 1877 along the Colorado Central Railroad, near its crossing of Big Thompson Creek. It was named for William S.H. Loveland, president of the railroad (of course!). The town initially depended on agriculture; its primary crops were sugar beets and sour cherries. In 1901, the Great Western Sugar Co. built its Loveland factory, which closed in 1985. During the 1920s, Loveland's Spring Glade orchard was the largest west of the Mississippi River, but by 1960, a series of droughts, blight and a killer freeze had destroyed the industry.

B STREET HOTEL: This hotel was operated by C. Davis in 1904.

LINCOLN HOTEL: Built before 1905, this hotel was located on the corner of Lincoln and Fourth Streets.

LOVELAND HOUSE: This hotel was operated by O. Riker in 1904.

Quarry workers stand outside the stone Stout Hotel, 1880s.

Stout (Under the Reservoir)

Stout, a former town in southern Colorado, was located in the foothills southwest of Fort Collins. Established in the 1880s as a camp for stone quarry workers, the town was abandoned in 1949 in anticipation of the inundation of the valley by the Horsetooth Reservoir.

STOUT HOTEL: Built sometime in the 1880s, the Stout Hotel was abandoned and razed in 1949.

TELLER COUNTY

A few years after gold was discovered at Cripple Creek, political differences between area miners and mine owners became so fierce that they caused the division of El Paso County. In 1899, Teller County was carved from the western slope of Pikes Peak and named after United States senator Henry Teller. Only five years after its formation, Teller County became the scene of the violent Colorado Labor Wars.

Cripple Creek

This fabled gold-mining town is located a few feet below timberline and surrounded by pasture. In 1890, Robert Miller Womack discovered rich ore in this previously unproductive region, instigating the last great Colorado gold rush. Thousands streamed into the region, and soon W.S. Stratton found the famous Independence Lode, one of the largest gold strikes in history. The district's gold was the core of an ancient volcano, six square miles in diameter. This geologic good fortune caused Cripple Creek's population to increase to ten thousand by 1893.

When the underground mines became exhausted, the town teetered on the brink of becoming a ghost town, though it has always had a few hundred faithful residents. With the passing of legalized gambling in 1991, Cripple Creek became a gambling and tourist town. Casinos have claimed many of its historic buildings.

When the mines gave out, many prospectors turned their burros loose. The hardy, four-legged creatures continued to thrive and reproduce in the wild over the years and once traveled the road between Cripple Creek and Victor in small packs. It was possible for motorists to encounter troops of them en route from one grazing area to another; they would pause to pet and feed burros through car windows. Bolder tourists ventured into the burro throng, making conversation and pictures. But a few years back, these burro pilgrimages were deemed unsafe for both burro and motorist, and the town rounded up the errant beasts. They are now kept in corrals until Donkey Derby Days, when the annual burro races are held through the streets of Cripple Creek. Burros have not been interviewed concerning this change in their circumstances.

Small herds of burros once traveled the road between Cripple Creek and Victor, circa 1972.

The Cripple Creek and Victor Narrow Gauge Railroad today operates from Cripple Creek and passes several small ghost towns and mines. Cripple Creek hosts many events throughout the year, including the Cripple Creek Ice Festival, Donkey Derby Days, the Fourth of July Celebration and Gold Camp Christmas.

HOTEL CARR: This hotel was built about 1892 and probably burned down in the 1895 town fire.

COMMERCIAL HOTEL: Built about 1892 on Bennett Avenue, the Commercial Hotel was destroyed in a town fire in 1896.

*HOTEL ST. NICHOLAS: 303 North Third Street, Cripple Creek, CO 80813; 719-689-0856; hotelstnicholas.com.

Built about 1898, this restored mountain inn occupies the elegant building once housing the St. Nicholas Hospital, operated by the Sisters of Mercy. Now listed on the National Historic Register, many of its furnishings and artifacts are original to the hotel and the fabled 1890s gold rush town of Cripple Creek.

IMPERIAL HOTEL: No information available.

NATIONAL HOTEL: Built in 1896, this hotel was razed in 1918. It was financed by a group of businessmen. It was located on the corner of Fourth and Bennett Avenue and was operated in 1904 by A.E. Willaber.

The hotel was elaborately furnished with mahogany and gilt, catering to mining magnates, railroad hierarchy and the upper crust of Cripple Creek society. Spencer Penrose, of BROADMOOR fame, reportedly rode on

Postcard of the Palace Hotel, circa 1895.

horseback into its bar—something he seems to have been particularly fond of doing. But the National's glory days were short lived, and the hotel began changing hands only a year after opening.

It struggled along for a while, renting rooms and showrooms to traveling salesmen, until its closing in 1918. With operating expenses too high to justify maintenance, the National was torn down that same year.

NEW COLLINS HOTEL: Built before 1904, this hotel was operated by M.E. Shoot

PALACE HOTEL: Built before 1895 on Bennett Avenue, this brick hotel withstood the 1905 fire.

PORTLAND HOTEL: Built sometime in the 1890s at 204 East Warren, in 1896 a grease fire in the kitchen destroyed the hotel and a large portion of the town that had survived a previous fire four days earlier.

Independence: Ghost Town

Established in 1881, Independence is now a ghost town sixteen miles east of Aspen. When the Independence Lode was discovered in 1879, a tent city sprang up, and by 1880, three hundred people lived in the camp. By 1882, the town of Independence had over forty businesses, with three post offices and approximately fifteen hundred residents.

CALIFORNIA HOTEL: Built about 1881, the California Hotel was abandoned in 1899. That year, the worst storm in Colorado's history cut off supply

California Hotel, circa 1885–90.

routes. The miners were running out of food, so they dismantled their homes to make seventy-five pairs of skis and escaped en masse to Aspen, leaving Independence a ghost town. Room and board cost two dollars at the New England House, a boardinghouse on the east end of Main Street and a competitor of the California Hotel. Today, the Aspen Historical Society preserves the town site and conducts tours.

Victor

Located five miles from Cripple Creek, Victor was established in 1893 and was known as the City of Mines for the richest mines in the Cripple Creek District on Battle Mountain, directly above town. Much of the mines' labor force made Victor home. It was also a rail and shipping center and later a milling center.

In August 1899, a devastating fire razed the town in less than five hours, but most of Victor's businesses rebuilt in brick in less than six months. The brick version of Victor has survived handsomely and is today a picturesque, historic mountain town.

Victor is the hometown of respected radio journalist and newspaperman Lowell Thomas. He spent his early years working at the *Victor Daily Record* and at the age of nineteen became its editor. Thomas later spent forty-six years on NBC's *Literary Digest* and in 1976 was awarded the Medal of Freedom by President Ford. The Victor Record building, where Thomas began his career, still stands on Fourth Street.

Though quiet today in contrast to its former days, Victor's rich past has begun to draw interested tourists and history buffs to the authentic atmosphere of this century-old mining town. Victor should not be missed.

HOTEL METROPOLE: Built by 1894, this hotel was destroyed in a 1899 citywide fire. *VICTOR HOTEL: 321 Victor Avenue, Victor, CO 80860; 716-689-3553, 800-713-4595; victorhotelcolorado.com.

This hotel was built between 1894 and 1899 at Fourth Street and Victor Avenue by the Woods family, the recognized founders of Victor. The original hotel was a two-story wooden frame building, which burned in the 1899 town fire. The hotel soon after moved across the street to the Woods' brick bank building.

During excavation for the hotel's foundation, a vein of gold ore was discovered, which led to the Gold Coin Mine. Victor, located almost ten thousand feet above sea level on the side of Battle Mountain, was destined to become a mecca for gold miners.

The Woods' First National Bank of Victor, the town's tallest building, was completed on Christmas Eve 1899, following the 1895 fire, which destroyed their bank at this location, as well as the wooden Victor Hotel across the street. In early years, the bank occupied the first floor, renting out upper floors as rooms and offices. Interestingly, while the bank was storing gold coins, miners in the Gold Coin Mine worked beneath it, as the mine's tunnels ran underneath downtown streets and buildings.

About 1906, the fourth floor was the town hospital, where surgery was performed. In winter, with the ground so frozen that graves could not be dug, its corner rooms were used as a morgue until warmer weather.

The Woods' bank was forced to close permanently in 1903, when bank examiners declared it insolvent. Several successor banks occupied the property, but all eventually closed, and the building remained vacant for many years. In 1992, the Woods' four-story brick building was renovated to become the new Victor Hotel, open again for business. The bank vault and original birdcage elevator, still in operation, can be seen from the hotel lobby. The Victor's "birdcage" is the oldest operating elevator in Colorado but was once the site of a tragedy.

Years back, a miner named Eddy lived in room 301 when the hotel operated as a boardinghouse. One fateful morning, Eddy rose for work,

The Hotel Victor today. *Photo courtesy of the Victor Hotel.*

pushed the button for the elevator and, when its iron gates opened, stepped inside—and fell to his death, the victim of the elevator's malfunction. Since then, there have been scattered reports of visitations by Eddy; room 301 is one of the most requested by ghost hunters.

Eddy's room is not the only thing visible from the third floor. The view of Victor's surrounding mountains is nothing short of spectacular. The landscape is so magnificent that Theodore Roosevelt, upon viewing the Sangre de Cristos and Western Range from Victor's Seventh Street location, is reported to have stated, "This is a view that bankrupts the English language."

The brick Hotel Victor stands opposite the site of its frame predecessor in the Victor National Historic District. The hotel is listed on the National Registry of Historic Places.

Woodland Park

Called the the "City Above the Clouds," Woodland Park is 8,465 feet above sea level. There is easy access to hiking, climbing and fishing in the area, as well as a new museum, the Rocky Mountain Dinosaur Resource Center.

CREST HOTEL: Built before 1904, this hotel was operated by S.A. Brown in 1904.
MIDLAND HOTEL: Built before 1904, this hotel was operated by Mrs. R.B. Hackman in 1904.
WOODLAND HOTEL: This hotel was built before 1904.

WELD COUNTY

The discovery of gold in 1858 along the South Platte River predated the Pikes Peak Gold Rush. Feeling separated from the distant territorial governments of Kansas and Nebraska, mining area residents voted to form the Territory of Jefferson in 1861. Jefferson Territory was never federally approved, but President Buchanan signed into law the Territory of Colorado. In November 1861, the Colorado General Assembly organized seventeen counties, including Weld, named for Lewis Ledyard Weld, lawyer and territorial secretary who died fighting for the Union army during the Civil War.

Greeley

This town began in 1869 as Union Colony, an experimental Utopian community "based on temperance, religion, agriculture, education and family values." It was founded by Nathan Meeker, an idealistic New York City reporter. He purchased property at the confluence of the Cache la Poudre and South Platte Rivers. Close to five hundred true believers made the journey west to establish the community, whose name was later changed to Greeley, for Horace Greeley, Meeker's editor at the *New York Tribune*.

In its early days, Greeley made use of thousands of roaming buffalo, which supported five businesses making buffalo robes. However, the arrival of open-range cattle, coming into town to graze gardens and crops, was less lucrative. So, in 1871, at the suggestion of Horace Greeley, a fifty-mile-long, seven-foot-high fence was constructed around the town. It had two gates that were locked from April through October, requiring people to unlock them in order to leave or access town. The fence created strife between farmers and cattlemen, some complaining that it was built to keep out "undesirables." Most of the fence was torn down by 1900.

The first sugar beet processing factory was built in 1902, and by the 1920s, Greeley was manufacturing 25 percent of the nation's sugar. The town's original colony placed strong emphasis on the arts, music and education, and Greeley is home to the oldest orchestra west of the Mississippi, the Greeley Philharmonic, begun in 1912.

In 1890, the State Normal School of Colorado opened its doors and is now the University of Northern Colorado.

CAMFIELD HOTEL: Formerly the Oasis Hotel, this hotel became the Camfield before 1910 and was owned by Daniel A. Camfield. In 1930, KFKA, Colorado's first commercial radio station, broadcast from the Camfield. The hotel was razed in the 1960s.

GREELEY HOUSE: This hotel was built before 1910.

OASIS HOTEL: Built before 1882, the Oasis became the Camfield Hotel about 1910.

STERLING HOTEL: This hotel was built before 1910.

HOTEL UNION: This hotel was built before 1904.

Longmont

In 1870, a group of prominent Chicago businessmen decided to start a new town in Colorado. Imagine that! They sold membership in the town, called

The Silver Moon Hotel was built sometime after 1872 at Third Avenue and Kimbark Street. Photo circa 1872.

the "Chicago-Colorado Colony," and bought sixty thousand acres of land in northern Colorado. By 1871, Longmont was built, named for nearby Long's Peak. The area's rich soil promoted agriculture. After the arrival of the Colorado Central Railroad in 1877, the community flourished, and a sugar factory, a cannery and a flour mill were constructed.

GERMANIA HOTEL: This hotel was operated by H.L. Hockberger in 1904.
GREAT WESTERN HOTEL: No information available.
IMPERIAL HOTEL: This hotel was operated by C.F. Allen in 1904.
SILVER MOON HOTEL: Built before 1872, this hotel was operated by T.J. Barker in 1904. The rate was one dollar per day. Its sign had a crescent-shaped moon symbol between "Silver" and "Hotel."

SOUTHEAST CENTRAL COUNTIES

After the gold and silver played out, untapped resources remained in the powerful draw of the land. Forests. Hot springs. Rivers. Majestic views. Eventually, even snow became a resource, and resorts of every stripe sprang up like crocuses. Some were splendid. Others only aspired to be. By the 1890s, there were hotels catering to every pocket and bank account.

Some of the more successful, which managed to avoid the flames of economic and actual conflagration, are still thriving today, more than a century later. Their survival is worthy of celebration; the loss of others is deserving of mourning. And there are some lesser establishments, long gone, that served their humble purpose in their day and are due a nod of recognition.

In this chapter are more historic hotels to acknowledge, mourn or celebrate.

ALAMOSA COUNTY

The first Europeans in Costilla County were Hispanic settlers from Taos, New Mexico, in 1851. Named for the Costilla River, Costilla was one of the original seventeen counties created in 1861. In 1913, Alamosa County was carved by the Colorado legislature from northwest Costilla County. Alamosa is a Spanish word meaning "grove of cottonwoods."

Hooper

Hooper is a tiny town in the San Luis Valley. Nearby points of interest include the Great Sand Dunes National Park and the contemporary UFO Watchtower, built by a local cattle rancher.

Commercial Hotel: Built before 1904, this hotel was operated by A.L. Jamison in 1904.
Hooper Hotel: Built before 1904, this hotel was operated by Mrs. J. Kipp in 1904.

Custer County

Custer County was created in 1877 and named for luckless Lieutenant Colonel Custer, killed the previous year. The county experienced a silver rush during the 1870s. Its county seat moved to Silver Cliff in 1886, before settling in Westcliffe in 1928.

Silver Cliff

Initially a silver boomtown, Silver Cliff is located in the Wet Mountain Valley. The first permanent settlers arrived in 1869; a year later, more than one hundred German families came from Chicago to homestead. As with all silver towns, fortunes fell as quickly as they rose. Once mining became unprofitable, ranching became the local mainstay.

Powell House Dining Room, 1881. This hotel got around.

When the Denver and Rio Grande Railroad arrived in 1881, it bought cheap land just west of Silver Cliff, in Westcliffe. This forced most businesses to relocate to Westcliffe, on land they had to buy from the railroad at inflated prices. Businessmen and homeowners put buildings on rollers and trundled them to Westcliffe, and by 1882, Silver Cliff's decline had begun. Today, it has repopulated into a quiet community.

POWELL HOUSE: Built before 1880. The hotel was later moved to Westcliffe, before 1904, and became the Westcliffe Hotel (see Westcliffe).
ST. CLOUD HOTEL: This hotel was taken to Cañon City when Silver Cliff declined.

Querida: Ghost Town

A silver mining town, Querida (Spanish for "beloved") was named for Edmund Bassick's highly productive local gold and silver mine. The town was also known as Bassick City. By 1882, the town's population was close to one thousand.

The Bassick Hotel goes up in flames, circa 1880s.

After clearing over $500,000 from his mine, Bassick sold out to New York investors, whose stingy management skills resulted in ore being smuggled out by disgruntled employees and sold in local saloons. The stolen ore was used to salt worthless claims, with the intention of selling the claims to gullible investors. The secret Querida Protective Society was formed to encourage this illegal fundraising and shield its members from the domineering mining company. When the Protective Society sent a threatening letter demanding that two Bassick mining officials be fired, the mining company responded by giving raises to the two men accused, and firing the men who sent the letter. A riot loomed on the horizon. Company supporters swore to decorate the trees with Protective Society members if they did not leave town immediately. Most departed quietly, and the rest were shipped out in a wagon and warned to never return. The mine closed in 1885; by 1906, the town was abandoned.

BASSICK HOTEL: Built before 1880s, this hotel burned down sometime in the 1880s.

Westcliffe

Westcliffe was built at the end of the new railroad tracks. Dr. William Bell, founder of Manitou Springs, and General Palmer, founder of Colorado Springs, planned the town before the railroad was completed. Named after Bell's hometown in England, Westcliffe drew the trade from Silver Cliff, emerging as the primary town in the Wet Mountain Valley.

POWELL HOUSE: Built before 1904, this hotel was operated by F. Sebelble in 1904. At some point, it became the Westcliffe Hotel.
WESTCLIFFE HOTEL: This hotel was operated by W.A. Hilton in 1904 (see Silver Cliff).
WOLFF HOTEL (aka the National Hotel): Built in 1887 by William Wolff at 209 South Second Street, this was Westcliffe's first hotel. It is still standing—the last remaining stone-front building in town.

EL PASO COUNTY

El Paso County is one of the original seventeen counties created in 1861 and was named for Ute Pass, north of Pikes Peak.

Calhan

At 6,535 feet above sea level, Calhan is reputedly the highest non-mountain town in the United States.

HOTEL CALHAN: This hotel was built sometime before 1906.

Cascade

Cascade, at 7,379 feet, was established in 1886 and was named for the area's many waterfalls. In 1889, the carriage road from Cascade was built to the top of Pikes Peak.

CASCADE HOUSE HOTEL: This hotel was built in 1887.
*EASTHOLME HOTEL: 4445 Hagerman Avenue, Cascade, CO 80809; 719-684-9901, 800-672-9901; info@eastholme.com.

An example of women's vision and foresight, the Eastholme Hotel was built in 1886 by well-to-do widow Eliza Marriott Hewlett of Schenectady, New York, and her sisters, Caroline and Ellen.

Considering the times in which these three women lived, the courage and determination required for such a venture was nothing less than heroic. But

Eastholme in the Rockies. *Photo courtesy of Eastholme in the Rockies.*

Hotel Ramona, a postcard of heartbreak for the historic hotel enthusiast.

Eliza Hewlett had assessed the area and wisely singled out Ute Pass as a prime target for tourism.

Though the sisters must have endured skepticism, they persevered, employing local craftsmen to build their eight-gabled establishment, designed after refined eastern hotels. Eliza also gave the name Cascade Canyon to the former Hurricane Canyon, now known as Cascade, Colorado. The Marriott women's dream came true and has survived for more than a century. Eastholme Hotel is a thriving bed-and-breakfast today, known as Eastholme in the Rockies.

HOTEL RAMONA: Built in 1889 and razed in 1924, this hotel was located on the Colorado Midland Railway. D.N. Heizer was the proprietor.

This massive Byzantine wonder rising out of the rugged Rockies, five miles from Manitou, was breathtaking to behold. With a domed tower and multiple verandas, the Ramona was a popular Ute Pass resort, located in Cascade Cañon. But it did not survive the ravages of time and poor economy.

Situated on Pikes Peak Road, the Ramona, named for a popular novel of the times, was a water stop for stagecoaches and railroads in the 1890s. Sadly, the grand, pastel-painted, three-story hotel suffered financially, as did many of its sister hotels, and was dismantled in 1924.

Green Mountain Falls

North of Pikes Peak and eleven miles west of Colorado Springs, at seventy-eight hundred feet, Green Mountain Falls nestles in a lush mountain valley,

A postcard of Green Mountain Falls Lake and Gazebo, with the hotel in the distance. The Green Mountain Falls Hotel was the strongest competition of the Hotel Ramona in Cascade, circa 1900.

surrounded by the Pike National Forest. The town's promotion began in 1887, once railroad access was established. Streets and a real estate office were constructed, and Green Mountain Falls Hotel was built above a man-made lake. Circus entrepreneur P.T. Barnum once had a summer home here. While the hotel is gone, the lake remains.

GREEN MOUNTAIN FALLS HOTEL: Built in 1899, this hotel burned down in 1908. It overlooked the lake, and the Colorado Midland Railway brought tourists by the thousands to watch balloon ascensions, hear band concerts and attend Saturday night dances.

TERRACE HOTEL: This hotel was built sometime before 1900.

Manitou Springs

Manitou Springs is tucked between the Garden of the Gods and Pikes Peak. William Blackmore, an English investor, suggested that "Manitou," a Native American word for spirit, was more appealing than "Villa la Font," the name given to the area by French trappers. The first major hotel, Manitou House, opened in 1872. Eleven mineral springs throughout town are fed by snowmelt from Pikes Peak. Long before white men arrived, the Ute, Arapahoe, Cheyenne and other native tribes considered the area sacred. By the early 1900s, the town was a health destination.

The source of Manitou's waters is a deep, underground system of aquifers. As water erodes surrounding limestone, carbonic acid is created, giving Manitou's springs their effervescence. This natural carbonation forces water through cracks in the rocks, where it absorbs high concentrations of sodium bicarbonate and other minerals.

Once the railroad spur arrived from Colorado Springs in 1881, Manitou expanded on a large scale. By the 1890s, the town had seven grand hotels, including Cliff House, Barker House and the Grandview, all of which still stand. Smaller hotels, boardinghouses and rental cottages became available to accommodate the visiting hordes. Guests arriving on the Denver and Rio Grande or Midland Railroads could bathe in the spring waters, soak in heated bathhouses and enjoy the town's many attractions, such as the Cog Railway, Rainbow Falls and the Cave of the Winds.

ARLINGTON HOTEL: Built before 1892, this hotel was operated by Mrs. C.T. Stevens in 1904.

BARKER HOUSE HOTEL: Built sometime in the 1870s or '80s, this hotel is still standing at 819 Manitou Avenue. It was purchased in 1904 by Charles Pollen and renamed the Navajo Hotel. The hotel hosted Wild Bill Cody and Theodore Roosevelt. It is now apartments and retail space.

BEEBEE HOUSE: Built about 1869 by F.W. Beebee, this was the first hotel in Manitou, with one hundred rooms.

A postcard of the Barker House, aka the Navajo Hotel, circa 1904.

BELLEVUE HOUSE: Built before 1904, this hotel was operated by Mrs. J.E. Laycock in 1904.

BONNIEBLINK: Built before 1904, this hotel was operated by Miss H. Frazier in 1904.

*CLIFF HOUSE: 306 Cañon Avenue, Manitou Springs, CO 80829; 719-685-3000; www.thecliffhouse.com.

Built in 1874, the Cliff House has been open longer than Colorado has been a state, compiling a fascinating history over its 125 years. The structure that became the twenty-room boardinghouse known as "the Inn" was originally a stagecoach stop on the route from Colorado Springs to Leadville.

Edward Nichols came west in the 1870s to cure his tuberculosis. Upon recovering, he moved to Manitou Springs and served eight terms as mayor. In 1886, he bought the Inn, renamed it Cliff House and began turning it into a sophisticated resort, emphasizing the region's mineral waters.

In 1914, Nichols collaborated with Colorado Governor Shoup and founded the Manitou Bath House Company, bringing specialized water therapies to the community. In the thirty years following, Nichols expanded the hotel from

The Cliff House today. *Photo courtesy of the Cliff House.*

twenty rooms to fifty-six, and eventually to two hundred. The result was a beautiful four-and-a-half-story building, looking much as it does today.

The hotel suffered two major disasters: a flash flood in 1921 and a ravaging fire in 1982, which forced the building to remain closed for sixteen years. In 1997, restoration began. The owner vowed to revive the hotel's original distinction and preserve the 1880s Rocky Mountain Victorian architecture, while incorporating twenty-first-century technology and amenities. After $10.5 million in labor and refurbishing, the vision has been realized.

The Cliff House Dining Room is AAA Four-Diamond rated and has won the "Best of Award of Excellence" from *Wine Spectator* magazine and the "Award of Unique Distinction" from Robert Parker's *Wine Enthusiast* magazine, for the hotel's wine list, which offers eight hundred selections (see Appendix A for selected dishes from the restaurant's exceptional menu).

Cliff House is on the National Registry of Historic Places.

CRAFTWOOD INN: This hotel was built about 1915.

DEERPATH LODGE: Built before 1904, this hotel was operated by Mr. Alp in 1904.

EAST LYNNE HOTEL: Built before 1904, this hotel was operated by W.J. Merwin in 1904.

A postcard of the Hidden Inn, circa 1920s. The back of the card states, "The Indian Pueblo shown here was erected by the Park Commission of Colorado Springs for the purpose of providing visitors to the Garden of the Gods with a resting place, where light refreshments could be served. The structure fits in between ledges of rocks, which appear to have been thrown up for the purpose. The building is of brick & concrete, covered with plaster made from the red sand and rocks, which are peculiar to the Garden of the Gods."

The second Iron Springs Hotel, built between 1886 and1901. It was operated by Miss L.G. Fellows in 1904. With sixty-five rooms, the Iron Springs Hotel was the first in the region to have its own water-powered turbine and electric lights.

GRAND VIEW INN: Built before 1904 at 935 Osage Avenue, this hotel was operated by William Paulson in 1904. It is still standing, now the home of the privately owned Summit Ministries.

HIDDEN INN: Near the Garden of the Gods, this hotel was built by the Colorado Springs Park Commission.

IRON SPRINGS HOTEL: Built between 1870 and 1885, a fire occurred in the rear of this hotel when a kerosene lamp exploded. According to the Manitou Fire Department, "That hotel was a rambling frame structure, built to burn." The hotel was rebuilt within a year.

MANITOU HOUSE: Built in 1872, this hotel burned down in 1903. It was located near the site of the Seven Minute Spring Pavilion. A three-story frame structure with a gabled roof, a central dormer, a wraparound porch and a balcony, its office featured hunting trophies, firearms and a safe. William Iles managed the hotel in 1875.

THE MANSIONS HOTEL: Built between 1875 and 1925, this hotel was operated by D.K. Torrey in 1904. In 1915, defective wiring caused the 104-room hotel to catch fire, with a loss of $70,000. Flames spread so rapidly that the entire building was soon a total loss. In 1924, following the hotel's rebuilding, it burned again. The Manitou Springs Fire Department put three lines of hose on it and called for help, but the fire had started in the basement, and the building's interior and roof were destroyed. The hotel was razed shortly thereafter.

NORRIS HOUSE: Built before 1904, this hotel was operated by J.A. Ray in 1904.
RED CRAGS LODGE: No information available.
RUXTON HOTEL: Built before 1904, this hotel was operated by F.M. Cooper in 1904.
SUNNY SIDE HOTEL: Built before 1904, this hotel was operated by W.H. Rogers in 1904.
SPRINGS HOTEL: Built in 1871, this hotel's proprietor was John N. Harden.

Monument

Situated on the Rampart Range in Northwest El Paso County, Monument, first called Henry's Station, was a stop along the Rio Grande Railroad in 1872.

MONUMENT HOTEL: Built before 1904, this hotel was operated by Mrs. H.S. Ballon in 1904.
RUPP HOTEL: Built before 1904, this hotel was operated by Dr. W.H. Rupp in 1904.

North Cheyenne Canyon

BRUIN INN: This hotel was built sometime between 1900 and 1907.

A postcard of the Bruin Inn.

Palmer Lake

Palmer Lake was established by General William Jackson Palmer in 1871. When Palmer founded Colorado Springs and started the Denver and Rio Grande Railroad, he purchased Monument Farms and Lake Property, now the Palmer Lake area. The railroad's steam trains had to fill with water to head down the Continental Divide, as the lake was the only convenient water supply. For a one-dollar round-trip fare from Denver, passengers could ride to Palmer Lake for a day of picnicking, fishing, boating or hiking. It is one of three communities in the Tri-Lakes Region between Denver and Colorado Springs, located off Interstate 25.

Dr. William Finley Thompson laid out the town in 1882 as a health and vacation resort. In 1887, Thompson, an oral surgeon from Ohio who had practiced in England and the Midwest, built his mansion, Estemere, in town. By 1890, he had to flee from creditors. Palmer Lake was a popular destination for those wishing to escape the city heat.

PALMER LAKE HOUSE: Built before 1904, this hotel was operated by R.W. Owens in 1904.
ROCKLAND HOTEL: Built before 1900, this hotel was operated by Mrs. J.W. Van Gilder in 1904. It was still in business in 1907.

A postcard of the Rockland Hotel, circa 1900.

Pikes Peak

Pikes Peak dominates the Front Range of the Rockies, ten miles west of Colorado Springs. It was named for Zebulon Pike, who led an expedition to southern Colorado in 1806. Pikes is 14,115 feet above sea level, one of Colorado's fifty-four 14,000-foot peaks. Pike declared that its top could never be reached, but botanist Edwin James ascended the summit in 1820. The first woman to climb the peak was Julia Holmes, in 1858. In 1889, a carriage road opened from Cascade, Colorado, to the top. Katherine Lee Bates wrote "America the Beautiful" in 1893, after traveling up the peak by carriage. A plaque at the top commemorates her work. In 1889, the Manitou and Pikes Peak Railway Company was founded, and in 1891, the first passenger train made it up Pikes. Baldwin Locomotive Works in Philadelphia, Pennsylvania, delivered three steam engines in 1890, and limited service began that year to Halfway House Hotel.

A postcard of the Pikes Summit Hotel with lookout tower, 1901.

An early postcard of the Halfway House Hotel, circa 1900.

HALFWAY HOUSE: This hotel was built before 1890.

PIKES SUMMIT HOTEL: This hotel was built before 1901. Spencer Penrose, who developed the BROADMOOR, eventually purchased the Cog Railway in the 1920s, reportedly to obtain the parking lot and Pikes Summit Hotel for auto travelers on the highway he had improved up the mountain.

FREMONT COUNTY

Fremont County is one of the seventeen original counties of the Colorado Territory. It was named for explorer Captain John Charles Fremont, known as "the Pathfinder." Fremont and his scout, Kit Carson, mapped the territory in 1843. Fremont County lies along the Arkansas River valley in south central Colorado, at the foot of the Rockies.

Cañon City

Cañon City was founded in 1858 during the Pikes Peak gold rush. It occupies both sides of the Arkansas River, but the first building was not constructed until 1860. The town offers historic interests, including dinosaur fossils, hot springs, the nearby Royal Gorge Canyon Bridge and the Colorado State Penitentiary.

CAÑON HOUSE: This hotel was built before 1920 on Main Street.

CENTRAL HOUSE/HOTEL: This hotel was built in 1899.

EL RIO HOTEL: This hotel was built before 1868 on the northwest corner of First Street.

HOT SPRINGS HOTEL/ROYAL GORGE HOT SPRINGS HOTEL: This hotel was built about 1873–74 by Dr. J.L. Prentiss. Prentiss, a local physician, purchased the hot springs, envisioning a health spa on the Arkansas River close to Royal Gorge. He first constructed a bathhouse and then a spacious frame hotel with a metal roof, a balcony-topped porch and a square tower housing the entry.

The tracks of the Denver and Rio Grande Railroad were across the river, and a swinging bridge was built for passengers to access the hotel. The business prospered briefly and was listed in the 1901 Cañon City Directory; it was not listed in 1905. A flood in 1916 took out the railroad and the hotel's trade with it. After a failed attempt at revival in the 1920s, the hotel sat vacant and was eventually razed in the 1940s.

MCCLURE HOUSE/STRATHMORE HOTEL: This hotel was built of local brick in 1874 at 323–31 Main Street by William H. McClure. Mrs. Maria Sheetz was the first manager. With sixty sleeping rooms, three suites and ten bathrooms, the McClure House drew a substantial clientele. In August 1900, the McClure House sold to English investors, who renamed it the Strathmore Hotel. They added an ornate reading room, spending $12,000 on velvet carpets, iron and brass beds and hardwood furniture. But time marches on, and the McClure House/Strathmore Hotel, though still standing, is currently Kate's Bar and Grill.

ST. CLOUD HOTEL: This hotel was built in 1888 at the corner of Seventh and Main Streets.

ST JAMES HOTEL: This hotel was built by 1904.

Florence

Florence, established in 1887, is set in the foothills of the Rockies on the picturesque Arkansas River. Its scenery drew the attention of early filmmakers when the Selig Film Company produced a silent western in 1910, starring cowboy star Tom Mix.

In 1871, the first Colorado Territory prison was built in the area, and since then, a large number of state and federal correction facilities have located in Fremont County.

FREMONT HOTEL: Built before 1904, this hotel was operated by H.L. Rice in 1904.

LENNOX HOTEL: This hotel operated from 1904 to 1924.

ROCK ISLAND HOTEL: Built before 1904, this hotel was operated by H. Killiam in 1904.

HUERFANO COUNTY

"Huerfano" translates to "orphan" in Spanish. This county, founded in 1861, was named for the Huerfano River and its local landmark, the Huerfano Butte, an isolated cone formation at the bottom of the river.

La Veta

Colonel John Francisco came to the Cuchara Valley in 1840, settling at Fort Garland until he built his plaza in La Veta, where he supplied settlers and gold miners. His plaza, which provided protection from Indian attack, is now Francisco Fort Museum. The railroad depot was built in 1876, and La Veta was incorporated.

CADILLAC HOUSE: Built before 1904, this hotel was operated by A. Larson in 1904.

COTTINGHAM HOTEL: Built before 1904, this hotel was operated by Craig and Reid in 1904.

DELAWARE HOUSE: Built before 1904, this hotel was operated by J.W. Calloway in 1904.

IVES HOTEL: Built before 1904, this hotel was operated by J.W. Ives in 1904.

LA VETA HOUSE: Built before 1904, this hotel was operated by N. Butterworth in 1904.

PAXTON HOUSE: Built before 1904, this hotel was operated by Mrs. Mary Paxton in 1904.

Walsenburg

Walsenburg is the county seat of Huerfano County. In 1870, Fred Walsen opened a large mercantile, drawing German settlers into the town. In his honor, the new town was named Walsenburg. In 1876, Walsen also opened the first coal mine. Coal mining strongly influenced the area for the next century.

Twin Lakes Hotel, 1893. The hotel burned down shortly after this photo was made.

Klein Hotel: Built before 1904 on Main Street, this hotel was operated by Mrs. H. Klein in 1904.

Oxford Hotel: This hotel was built before 1910.

Twin Lakes Hotel: Built in 1887 by Martin and Holmes in Garden City (a quarter mile away), the hotel was later moved to this location. It was operated by L.B. Countryman in 1904.

Walsenburg House: This hotel was built before 1904.

Las Animas County

Las Animas County, founded in 1866, is named for the Mexican title of the Purgatoire River, originally called El Rio de las Animas Perdidas en Purgatorio, or the "River of the Lost Souls in Purgatory."

Trinidad

Founded in 1862, Trinidad was officially established in 1872. Bat Masterson was town marshal in 1882, before moving to Colorado's backcountry. While here, the Earps and Doc Holliday joined Masterson in Trinidad, direct from their shootout at the OK Corral.

ADELPHIA HOTEL: Built sometime in the 1880s, likely by I.H. Rapp, this hotel was located on North Commercial Street.

CARDENAS HOTEL: Built in 1903 and razed in 1933, the Cardenas was a two-story, L-shaped, Mission-style stucco structure with a red tiled roof and an arcaded porch. A two-story building to the west housed a laundry and employee rooms. The Cardenas was located near the Atchison, Topeka and Santa Fe Railroad Depot. In 1904, the Purgatoire/Las Animas River flooded, destroying the depot but leaving the hotel intact. By 1905, a new depot had been built to resemble the Cardenas and was connected to the hotel by a colonnade.

The Cardenas was part of the chain of Harvey House hotels along the Santa Fe Railway. In 1889, Fred Harvey obtained exclusive rights to operate his eating-houses and hotel facilities on Santa Fe railroads west of the Missouri River. Harvey Houses, known for first-class food, service and cleanliness, were completely staffed by women, known as Harvey Girls.

In 1883, offended by customers' appalling behavior toward the predominantly black staff, who were frequently obliged to carry guns for protection, Harvey decided to hire only female waitresses. He advertised in newspapers for single, educated young women, between the ages of eighteen and thirty, "of good character, attractive, and intelligent." The girls were paid $17.50 a month, plus room, board and tips.

A postcard of the Cardenas Hotel. Built in the Mission style along the banks of the Purgatoire/Las Animas River, the hotel was a two-story structure with an arcaded porch, a terra-cotta roof, a balcony and porticos. Signs over its twin entrances read: "Cardenas."

The girls adhered to a 10:00 p.m. curfew, administered by a housemother. Their starched black-and-white uniform consisted of a skirt no more than eight inches off the floor, a stiff apron, a high collar and black stockings and shoes—all intended to diminish the figure. Hair was netted and tied with a plain white ribbon, and makeup and chewing gum were prohibited.

The Cardenas played a significant role in Trinidad's history during the railroad era (1870–1945), but it closed in 1933 and was demolished. The depot operated until 1960, when it, too, was razed, replaced by a new depot that is still in use. No visible evidence of the Cardenas remains. Its general location has been determined via Sanborn Fire Insurance Maps, showing the former hotel's west wing as located beneath the present depot. The Cardenas site is in the Corazon de Trinidad Historic District, listed on the National Register of Historic Places.

COLORADO HOTEL: This hotel was built before 1867 on Main Street.

GRAND UNION HOTEL/COLUMBIAN HOTEL: This hotel was built in 1878 by John Conkie as the Grand Union at the corner of Main and Commercial Streets.

Conkie was the owner, architect and builder of the Grand Union, but a game of poker reportedly cost him his hotel. Conkie's lost baby was a three-story, elaborately painted and decorated structure with nearly one hundred rooms. In the early 1880s, an elevator was installed. By the 1890s, the hotel was known as the Columbian.

Years prior to the hotel's construction, "Red" Bransford, a relative of Crazy Horse and sister of Oglala Sioux chief Red Cloud, operated an early lodging establishment on this very site.

In 1913, the state militia occupied the Columbian during the violent labor strike in nearby Ludlow. Miners, offended by militia presence, picketed the hotel, but once the strike was settled, they could again be found drinking in the Columbian's bar and gambling in its basement. Local urban legend says that actor Tom Mix occupied room 214, while his horse slept in room 212.

The building was restored in 1997 and is currently retail space. Located in the Corazon de Trinidad National Historic District, it is a prominent structure on Trinidad's downtown walking tour.

HOTEL CORINADO: Built before 1914 at the corner of Church and Commercial Streets, this hotel burned down in the 1980s.

DENVER HOTEL: This hotel was built in 1882 in the 200 block of North Commercial Streets. Pietro Mauro was thought to be the owner.

DULING LODGE: This hotel was built before 1900.

HOTEL GILMORE: This hotel was built before 1914.

MAIN HOTEL: This hotel was built about 1900 on a lot owned by Jennie Henry.

The carved mahogany bar of the Columbian, circa 1880s. Bat Masterson, Trinidad's town marshal in the 1880s, gambled in the basement here with Wyatt Earp and Doc Holliday and had a drink or two—or three.

NEW METROPOLITAN HOTEL: This hotel was built before 1914.
TOLTEC HOTEL: Built about 1910–11 in the 100 block of North Commercial Street, this hotel was constructed by F. E. Edbrooke Architectural Company, builders of the Tabor Opera House Block and the Denver Brown Palace. After falling into disrepair, the Toltec narrowly escaped the wrecking ball and has been renovated into shops and apartments.
TRINIDAD HOTEL: This hotel was built in 1900 at 421 North Commercial Street.

OTERO COUNTY

This county, taken from the western part of Bent County, was named for Miguel Otero. The Oteros, an old Spanish family from New Mexico, owned the mercantile firm of Otero, Sellars & Co. and founded La Junta.

La Junta

La Junta, "The Junction" in Spanish, was founded in 1875, as a temporary stopping point of the Atchison, Topeka and Santa Fe Railroad. In 1878, the

A postcard of the Santa Fe Hotel, circa 1913.

Santa Fe expanded to Trinidad but built a depot, roundhouses and repair shops in La Junta to make it the headquarters of the Colorado division. La Junta's economy is primarily based on agriculture, cattle and rail transportation.

HALLWAY HOTEL: This hotel was operating before 1904.
LA JUNTA HOTEL: Built in 1882, the La Junta Hotel also held a railroad eating-house, El Otero, run by Fred Harvey. The hotel closed in 1948.
SANTA FE HOTEL: Built before 1910.

Manzanola

This small agricultural community takes its name from the Spanish word for apple.

MANZANOLA HOTEL: Built before 1904, this hotel was operated by R.R. Baldwin in 1904.

Rocky Ford

At an elevation of 4,178 feet in the Arkansas Valley, this small community lies east of Pueblo. The town's name reportedly comes from the spot in the Arkansas River where settlers crossed to avoid quicksand. The town is home of the Rocky Ford cantaloupe and is known as the Melon Capital of the World. The annual Arkansas Valley Fair is held in August, celebrating the diverse culture with horse races, stock shows, a carnival and a rodeo. Some of Rocky Ford's farming success can be attributed to settler George Swink, who convinced neighbors to build the valley's first community irrigation system, transforming Rocky Ford into a top agricultural area. Swink shipped watermelons and cantaloupe as far as New York City in the late 1800s and is credited with introducing the commercial growing of fruit and vegetables in the United States. By exposing Rocky Ford melons to distant locales, Swink helped establish the melon's lasting fame.

EL CAPITAN HOTEL: This hotel was built before 1904.
ST. JAMES HOTEL: This hotel was built before 1904.

PUEBLO COUNTY

Pueblo County, formed in 1861, was named for the city of Pueblo, Colorado, the Spanish word for "town."

Old Colorado City

Old Colorado City, established in 1861, was built on a shaky boundary line, sometimes disputed, between the Sioux, Arapaho and Cheyenne of the Plains and their historic enemies, the mountain Utes. This made for some interesting negotiating—or lack thereof—when white settlers arrived. The town was once a drinker's paradise during local prohibition, until it was annexed in 1917, becoming the west side of Colorado Springs.

EL PASO HOUSE (aka Holmes House, Baird & Smith Hotel): This hotel was built about 1860.
HOFFMAN HOUSE: Built before 1888 and located in a row of two-story businesses, this hotel was operated by N.B. Hames in 1904.
NATIONAL HOTEL: Built before 1904, this hotel was operated by T. Ensign.

Colorado Springs

Located at the foot of Pikes Peak, this town was established in 1871 by General William Palmer with the intention of creating a high-quality resort community. It was soon nicknamed "Little London."

By 1904, Colorado Springs had one-third of the nation's one hundred millionaires, derived from Cripple Creek gold. Its dry climate was beneficial to tuberculosis sufferers, and many sanitariums sprang up in the area.

In 1899, Nikola Tesla began research in a lab located near Foote Avenue and Kiowa Street, where there was room for his high-voltage, long-distance, wireless transmission–reception experiments. Here, Tesla observed unusual signals that he later thought could be evidence of extraterrestrial radio communications from nearby planets. Tesla left town in January 1900; his lab was torn down about 1905, and its contents were sold. The Colorado experiments prepared Tesla for establishing the transatlantic wireless telecommunications facility known as Wardenclyffe.

HOTEL ACACIA: Built before 1890 on Platte Avenue, this hotel was still operating in the 1940s.

THE ALAMO HOTEL: Built before 1904, this hotel was operated by G.S. Elstun.

ALTA VISTA HOTEL: Built about 1889, this hotel was operated by H.H. Stevens in 1904.

THE ANTLERS HOTEL: This hotel was built in 1883 by General Palmer, who named the hotel for his extensive collection of deer and elk trophies displayed there. When English professor Katharine Lee Bates stayed at the first Antlers Hotel in 1893, she took a horse and buggy to the top of Pikes Peak. That journey inspired her famous anthem, "America the Beautiful." But the elaborately gabled, turreted building, furnished with leather furniture and rare carpeting, burned down in the fall of 1898.

Palmer's first Antlers Hotel, circa 1883.

A postcard of the second Antlers Hotel, circa 1890s. This east façade view features a U-shaped plan, with a porte-cochère, an arcaded porch, pediments, square towers with arcaded lookouts, chimneys, arched windows and a solarium.

Palmer engaged the firm of Varian and Sterner to design a more elaborate Antlers. The enormous new hotel opened in 1901, featuring two hundred rooms, three stone stairways, mosaic floors, tapestries and all the trappings money could buy. The hotel provided ample opportunities for sports interests, including coyote hunts and automobile trips. It was immediately successful, drawing the rich and famous, as well as Presidents Harrison, Harding, Taft and the ever-ebullient Theodore Roosevelt, who gave a speech from its balcony.

But the Antlers, for all its elegance and appeal, offended some in its high-handed dealings, one of whom was the ubiquitous Spencer Penrose, whose shenanigans on horseback in the Antlers' bar prompted his eviction. At the time, Penrose vowed to build a resort to put the Antlers to shame. And he did: the BROADMOOR.

Although it gradually fell from favor, the Antlers continued to operate until the Second World War. It was eventually torn down in 1964, following another fire. In recent years, the Hilton chain has obtained the property, building the large, contemporary Antlers Hilton at 4 South Cascade Avenue, near the original site.

*THE BROADMOOR: 1 Lake Avenue, Colorado Springs, CO 80906; 719-577-5775, 866-837-9520; www.broadmoor.com.

Before it was the Broadmoor Dairy Farm, the land at the base of Cheyenne Mountain was a ranch where corn was grown for making brooms. In 1880, Willie Wilcox, who came west seeking fortune and a cure for tuberculosis, bought the land and established the Broadmoor Dairy. He sold it in 1890 to Count Pourtales, who formed the Broadmoor Land and Investment Company. To entice the sale of lots, Pourtales built the Broadmoor Casino in 1891. A small hotel was constructed a few years later.

Enter Spencer Penrose, a Philadelphia entrepreneur who had made his fortune in gold and copper mining. In 1916, he purchased the Broadmoor Casino and Hotel and its forty-acre site, plus an adjoining four hundred acres. Penrose had recently undertaken a new project—to turn the Pikes Peak region into a multifaceted resort area. Architectural features of Penrose's "new" resort included a spectacular curved marble staircase, dramatic chandeliers, Della Robbia–style tile, hand-painted beams and ceilings, a carved marble fountain and a striking pink stucco façade.

Under the guiding hand of Penrose and his wife, Julie, the BROADMOOR resort opened in 1918 with three buildings, 350 rooms and a golf course designed by Donald Ross. A self-styled rustic rowdy, Penrose was an anti-prohibitionist of renown. In 1920, shortly after the BROADMOOR opened, Penrose brought fifty-five top hoteliers and five press people by private train from New York to Colorado Springs to show off his property. His invitations advised guests to bring "five bottles of your favorite cologne." Drinkable, of course. He also had a flatbed car on the train, guarded by a U.S. marshal; the flatbed contained what Penrose called his "gasoline."

Next to the Tavern Restaurant on the lobby level is one of the hotel's most famous spots: Bottle Alley, containing many bottles from Prohibition, mostly consumed by the Penroses and their guests over the years. A closer look reveals bottles on which Penrose wrote where the drink was consumed and who drank it with him. But there is one bottle, not from Prohibition days, signed by George W. Bush on his fortieth birthday. It was reportedly the last time the former president imbibed.

As the current manager was walking through the basement with maintenance staff, he spotted a small door partially hidden behind filing cabinets. No one knew where it led. They moved cabinets, broke a lock and were nearly knocked down by the smell of rotting hay and fermentation. It seems the wily Penrose had hidden three flatcars of alcohol in the tunnels that ran from the original casino to houses of ill repute located across the street in the early days. Apparently, he either forgot them after the repeal of Prohibition or neglected to tell anyone they were there before he died in 1939. Some bottles were bad; others were kept by the hotel as part of its collection.

Back in the 1950s, on break from filming in Arizona, John Wayne was a BROADMOOR guest. Staff members told about taking a banquet tray of shrimp up an elevator to one of the suites. They found Wayne on the elevator, and as they rode together, Wayne kept eating the shrimp. The servers reached their floor with a half-eaten tray for the party. As they prepared to explain to the guests that they would get a new tray, Wayne took over, pushed the tray into the room and, in his distinctive voice, announced, "Here's your tray, and I ATE the shrimp." No one complained. Wayne had more shrimp sent up and then stayed to sign autographs.

The grand resort has long been the destination of presidents, statesmen, foreign dignitaries and celebrities. Presidents Hoover, Franklin D. Roosevelt, Eisenhower, Kennedy, Nixon, Ford, Reagan and George H.W. and George W. Bush have all stayed at the BROADMOOR. It has hosted King Hussein of Jordan, Princess Anne, Prime Minister Toshiki Kaifu of Japan, the King of Siam and Margaret Thatcher, as well as celebrities Maurice Chevalier, Bing Crosby, Walt Disney, Charles Lindbergh, Clark Gable, Bob Hope, Jimmy Stewart, Jack Benny, Jackie Gleason, Sir Elton John, Ted Turner, Jane Fonda, Michael Douglas, Joe DiMaggio, Stan Musial, Sugar Ray Leonard, Stephen Tyler and Aerosmith, to name a few.

Legends linger about what prompted Penrose to build the BROADMOOR. Some insist that he built it out of spite, after the Antlers' management rebuked him for riding his horse into their bar. Others believed he and MacNeill built the hotel so they could hire their friend William Dunning, who had been fired from the Antlers. It is also said that the little "a" in BROADMOOR was meant as an insult to the Antlers. Regardless of the actual facts, it would seem that Penrose lost little love on the stodgy Antlers. But the name's unique styling also created a logo that could be trademarked, since "Broadmoor" had already been copyrighted.

The BROADMOOR has over seven hundred rooms, eighteen restaurants and cafés, three golf courses, a world-class spa and the Carriage House Museum. The hotel is still known as the "Grand Dame of the Rockies," with fine cuisine and entertainment, elegant appointments and Italian Renaissance–style architecture.

The BROADMOOR is the longest-running consecutive winner of both the AAA Five-Diamond and the Forbes/Mobil Travel Guide Five-Star Awards. Among its eighteen award-winning restaurants are the Penrose Room, for over

A postcard of a Maxfield Parrish painting of the BROADMOOR.

fifty years one of the region's top destinations for classic fine dining; Charles Court, specializing in American cuisine; the Summit, an American Brasserie, designed by renowned architect Adam D. Tihany; the Tavern, since 1938, serving hand-cut prime steaks, chops, seafood and prime rib in the original Tavern room, the Art Deco–era Mayan Room or the glass-enclosed Garden Room; the Golden Bee, which came to the BROADMOOR in 1961 as a collection of panels and fixtures from a nineteenth-century pub, shipped from England and reassembled in Colorado Springs, the town once nicknamed "Little London"; and the original Lake Terrace Dining Room, with views of Cheyenne Lake and the mountains, offering Eggs Benedict, Rocky Mountain trout, Continental and Southwestern specialties. A Sunday buffet with ice sculptures features more than seventy items; dessert selections are highlighted by its famous Bananas Foster and decadent Chocolate Fountain.

Among the resort's other fine restaurants are the Golf Club Dining Room, the Grille at the Golf Club, the Spa Café, Main Pool Café, Espresso BROADMOOR, Café Julie, Mountain Clubhouse and Oasis.

COLORADO SPRINGS HOTEL: This hotel was built in 1872 on Cascade Avenue by General William Palmer, who invited William Iles to come from England as manager. When Iles disagreed with Palmer over the sale of alcohol, his stay was short lived.

Colorado Springs Hotel, circa 1875.

ELK HOTEL: This hotel was built before 1900 at Pikes Peak Avenue and was operated by C.E. Tyler in 1904.

JOYCE HOTEL: Located at 10 South Weber Avenue, this hotel was operated by E.R. Joyce. Sepia postcards of the Joyce Hotel promise that it is "Modern, Clean, Homelike. Adjacent New Post Office. Best Location and Best Accommodations for the Money. With or Without Meals. Centrally Located."

PLAZA HOTEL: This hotel was built before 1910.

RED ELK HOTEL: This hotel was built before 1900.

ROCK ISLAND HOTEL: This hotel was built sometime between 1890 and 1900.

SPAULDING HOTEL: Built before 1904, this hotel was operated by J.A. Himebaugh in 1904.

Pueblo

In 1842, Fort Pueblo was established near the confluence of the Fountain and Arkansas Rivers. Built mainly of adobe, "El Pueblo" was a trading center on the border between Mexico and the United States. On December 24, 1854, Indians attacked the fort, killing everyone. Local ranchers buried the victims, and then the area was abandoned for years. When gold and silver were discovered on the Arkansas River, Pueblo was reestablished as a town, and by 1870, it had a population of 2,265.

Pueblo is the hometown of writer Damon Runyon and Dutch Clark, the first Colorado man in the NFL Hall of Fame. The Historic Arkansas River Project (HARP), a downtown river walk in the Union Avenue Historic Commercial District, restored the Arkansas River to its original channel and recounts the devastating 1921 Pueblo Flood, when fifteen hundred people were drowned.

CLARK'S WELLS HOTEL: Built before 1904, this hotel was operated by Clark & Brainard in 1904.

COMMERCIAL HOTEL: This hotel was built before 1900.

CONGRESS HOTEL: Built before 1900, this hotel incorporated the former Grand Hotel as its North Wing about 1900 (see Grand Hotel).

FARGO HOTEL: This hotel was built before 1900.

FARRISS HOTEL: Placed on the National Register of Historic Places in 1985, this hotel was removed from the registry and demolished in 1991.

FIFTH AVENUE HOTEL: This hotel was built before 1890.

GRAND HOTEL: Built before 1887 at Eighth and Santa Fe Streets, this hotel was razed in 1961. It was owned by J.P. Whitney in 1887 and changed its name to the Imperial about 1904. Later, it became the North Wing of the Congress Hotel. The Grand featured a four-story rotunda with a stained-glass ceiling and a cast-iron, calla lily fountain rising from a pool in the center. Its one hundred sleeping chambers, dining room and billiard room were of the highest caliber (see Congress and Imperial Hotels).

IMPERIAL HOTEL: The second name by which the Grand Hotel was called, this hotel was operated by Miller & Babne in 1904.

HOTEL MAINE: Built before 1903, this hotel was operated by W.A. Arey in 1904.

ROYAL HOTEL: Built before 1904, this hotel was operated by Mrs. A. Royal in 1904.

SOUTHERN HOTEL: Built before 1904, this hotel was operated by Charles Kresham in 1904.

UNION STATION HOTEL: Built before 1904, this hotel was operated by E.A. Thayer in 1904.

HOTEL VAIL: Built in 1911 at 217 South Grand Avenue, on the corner of Grand and Union Avenues, this hotel was named for Pueblo newspaperman John F. Vail. It is listed on the National Register of Historic Places as part of the Union Avenue Historic Commercial District. It is not currently in use.

VICTORIA HOTEL: This hotel was built before 1880 on northwest corner of "B" Street and Victoria Avenue.

Rye

Rye is a lovely little community in the eastern foothills of the Wet Mountains.

WILSON HOUSE: This hotel was built before 1913.

A postcard of the Wilson House, 1913.

WEST CENTRAL COUNTIES

Mining towns were rough, and facilities were nonexistent. Weather in the high country is always unpredictable, and getting lumber and supplies to remote locations was a considerable challenge. Some of the hotels pictured in this book attest to that, yet the pictures also remind us that some indomitable soul took it upon him (or her) self to try and make a go of it in a most unwelcome landscape. Miners needed food, heat and a bed. The heat may have been iffy, but two out of three wasn't bad, and these rustic innkeepers supplied all they could. Their crudely built structures, daring to proclaim themselves hotels, are testimony to the frontier spirit. Or to quote a movie of more recent years, "If you build it, they will come."

Gold and silver were the two elements that built the West, and Colorado was no exception. Fortunes rose and fell with the silver boom and the silver crash. The Pikes Peak gold rush saw many fortunes rise and just as many "bust," but the gambling halls rolled on, regardless of the season. One might lose all due to bad luck, poor judgment or a collapsing economy, but there was still a chance of restoration through cards and roulette wheels. This controversial layer of socioeconomic activity brought more visitors into the towns, further increasing the need for housing and stimulating the building industry as more hotels were constructed.

Gold mines sprang up in the Rockies like aberrant prairie dog holes. As civilization surrounded the mines, towns like Victor, Cripple Creek, Golden and Leadville were born. Hotels celebrated the discovery of rich ores with names like Gold Coin Inn, La Veta (the Vein) and Eureka House.

Colorado remembers those exciting days and reveals them to us in its remaining old hotels and inns, many of which are still in operation. Buildings tell the stories of those who built them and those who stayed within. As the reader browses through this book, let the pictures and descriptions stir the imagination, drawing the mind back in time to a lively and exhilarating era when men and women staked their claims on strata of society just as miners did on gold and silver.

ALAMOSA COUNTY

Alamosa County was created by the Colorado legislature in 1913 from northwestern Costilla County. Alamosa is the Spanish word for "grove of cottonwood trees."

Alamosa

Established in 1878 by the Denver and Rio Grande Railroad, this town became an important rail center. The city takes its name from the Alamosa River and is the county seat.

BROADWELL HOUSE: This hotel was built before 1907 on South Sixth Street.
ELKS HOTEL: This hotel was built sometime before 1904.
ST. CHARLES HOTEL: This hotel was built sometime before 1904.
VICTORIA HOTEL: Built before 1904 on State Street, this hotel was a two-story stone building with a corner entrance.

ARCHULETA COUNTY

Archuleta County has been home to the Anasazi, the Ute, the Navajo and the Apache. The area was first claimed for Spain by early Spanish explorers, and after the Mexican revolution, it became part of the Territory of Northern Mexico. Following the war with Mexico in 1848, it became the United States' possession. When Congress recognized the Colorado Territory in 1861, this area was designated part of Conejos County. In 1885, Archuleta County was created from western Conejos County and named for Antonio D. Archuleta, senator from Conejos County at the time.

Pagosa Springs

Pagosa Springs, at an elevation of 7,108 feet, is named after the Great Pagosa Hot Springs. Describing the boiling, bubbling alkaline spring, ancient Utes called it Pah-gosa: "pah" meaning water and "gosa" meaning boiling. Modern advertising has changed the meaning to "healing waters."

About 1867, the Utes gained control of the Great Spring from the Navajos, but their control was relatively short lived. The Brunot Agreement of 1874 signed the springs over to the white man. Three bands of the original seven that make up the Ute tribe are still located in the Pagosa area.

The military established an army post in the vicinity, choosing the Great Pagosa Hot Springs for its site. In 1878, Camp Lewis, later Fort Lewis, was built on the west bank of the San Juan River, opposite the Great Spring. Six square miles centering on the spring were declared a military reservation in 1879.

With the presence of the fort, more settlers began moving in. Fort Lewis remained in Pagosa Springs until early 1880, when it was moved to the banks of the La Plata River. The remaining outpost was designated Camp Pagosa Springs.

As word of the hot springs spread, people came to partake of the reported medicinal mineral waters. Pioneers settled the area by the early 1880s, raising cattle, sheep, grains and vegetables. They established businesses, and bathhouses sprang up around the Great Hot Spring like mushrooms. Pagosa Springs was incorporated in 1891, and its commercial district was located on the San Juan River. The area is known for its abundant fishing and hunting.

AMERICAN HOTEL: Built before 1904, this hotel was operated by Mrs. L.T. Harris in 1904.

COMMERCIAL HOTEL: Built before 1904, this hotel was operated by Mrs. Cora Seavey in 1904.

LOS BANOS HOTEL: This hotel was operating in 1920.

METROPOLITAN HOTEL: This hotel was built before 1915.

NICKLE PLATE HOTEL: Built before 1904, this hotel was operated by W. Glassner in 1904.

PATRICK HOTEL: Built before 1904, this hotel was operated by M.A. Patrick in 1904.

SAN JUAN HOTEL: Built before 1904, this hotel was operated by Mrs. Cade in 1904.

SPRINGS HOTEL: Built before 1904, this hotel was operated by W.B. Alexander in 1904.

STRAWN HOTEL: Built before 1904, this hotel was operated by A.L. Strawn in 1904.

CHAFFEE COUNTY

Chaffee County, located on the eastern slope of the Rockies in southwest central Colorado, has more fourteen-thousand-foot peaks that any other county and has been called the "Fourteener Region." Chaffee was created by the Colorado legislature in 1879 from southern Lake County and was named for Jerome B. Chaffee, Colorado's first United States senator.

Alpine: Partial Ghost Town

This small former mining community, founded in the 1870s, is often considered a ghost town. When the mines gave out, both Alpine and nearby St. Elmo became ghost towns. Although a few hardy residents continued to stay on, both towns remained nearly empty for fifty years. In the 1950s, people began building summer homes in Chalk Creek Gulch and fixed up some of the salvageable buildings in Alpine and St. Elmo. Current residents are respectful of the community histories, taking pride in maintaining the character of these two old mining towns. The San Isabel National Forest surrounds both Alpine and St. Elmo.

Alpine's first cabin was built in 1877, and by 1880, its population was five hundred. The town, a supply center for other towns along Chalk Creek, had two hotels, a dance hall, twenty-three saloons and a newspaper. When the railroad

The Badger Hotel, 1881. This hotel was named for the Badger State of Wisconsin, the home state of owners Captain Ford and John T. Swain.

extended to St. Elmo, the life was drawn away from Alpine. The newspaper, banks and most businesses moved to St. Elmo, taking the people with them and making Alpine another example of the railroad's power during that era.

BADGER HOTEL: This hotel was built before 1881.

Buena Vista

Unlike the mining towns, Buena Vista boasts a reputedly peaceable history, though it was reported to have had, at one time, three dozen bars and a hanging judge. It was settled in 1864, incorporated in 1879 and became a railroad town serving the local mining industry. The town has long been acknowledged for its mineral hot springs and excellent river rafting nearby.

AMERICAN HOUSE: This hotel was built before 1904.
*BUENA VISTA/COTTONWOOD HOT SPRINGS HOTEL: The Buena Vista was built in 1878 by Reverend J.A.D. Adams and his wife, a physician, as a hotel and sanitarium treating rheumatism and dyspepsia. The waters, 132 to 150 degrees, were piped into the house for drinking, bathing and treatments. The main house held the office, library, parlor and private rooms, with additional

A postcard of the Buena Vista Hot Springs Hotel, prior to its razing by fire in 1911. Today, it is known as the Cottonwood Hot Springs in Buena Vista.

sleeping and bathing quarters in the wings. The property was owned by Gabe Durst in 1911 when the hotel burned down. It was not rebuilt.

The hot springs are still open as Cottonwood Hot Springs (18999 County Road 306, Buena Vista, CO 81211; 719-395-6434). The resort offers a variety of spa treatments and overnight accommodations.

CAPITOL HOTEL: This hotel was built before 1890.

HAYWOOD HOTEL: This hotel was built sometime before 1904 and was operated by Mrs. W.W. Dickey in 1904.

HORTENSE HOTEL: Built before 1904, this hotel was operated by H.C. Johnson in 1904.

LAKE HOUSE HOTEL: This hotel was built before 1879.

*MT. PRINCETON HOT SPRINGS/HOTEL: Begun in 1879, this hotel was dismantled in 1950. It was originally a three-story hotel called the Antero, which did not prosper due to incompetence and bad management. Construction was begun in 1879 but was not completed until about 1910. In 1913, the hotel sold to the Carlsbad Hot Springs Corporation, which also failed to make it prosper, and it changed hands again in 1915. The new owners added a fourth floor to the hotel and two massive towers. Guests were offered large rooms with marble fixtures, copper tubs, hardwood floors, paneling, elaborate stairs and stained glass.

More than seven hot springs bubbled behind the hotel, and an elaborate bathhouse was constructed to accommodate bathers. By the early 1920s, management of the Mt. Princeton Hot Springs/Hotel seemed to have finally found the formula for success. Its moment in the sun lasted almost ten years. Unfortunately, the last mine closed in 1924, the railroad removed its tracks in 1926 and the Great Depression sounded doom for resorts across the country. The hotel changed hands some more until 1950, when John Crowe bought the hotel, took it apart and used its more than one million board feet of lumber to build a subdivision in Texas. An ignominious end for a noble lady.

The Heywood Springs at the mouth of Chalk Creek were used for centuries by Native Americans and visited by white settlers in the 1860s. They were later developed, and today there are three large pools open to the public. Water in these pools enters at about 133 degrees and is kept around 95 degrees in winter and a bit cooler in summer. Other hot springs in the area include Hortense Hot Springs, not far from the Mt. Princeton pools. At 185 degrees, this pool is thought to be the hottest geothermal spring in the state. The springs are known today as the Mt. Princeton Hot Springs Resort (15870 County Road 162, Nathrop, CO 81236; 719-395-2447, 1-888-395-7799).

PRINCETON HOTEL: Built before 1903, this was a frame hotel with brick chimneys, dormer windows and a rounded turret with a conical dome. A dammed lake with falls at the City Park was next to the hotel grounds.

Poncha Springs

Tucked into a valley and surrounded by the San Isabel National Forest, Poncha Springs calls itself the "Crossroads of the Rockies." From the area's plentiful hot springs and the influence of Spanish culture, the site was originally called Poncho—"cape" for warmth—Springs. In 1924, the town renamed itself Poncha Springs.

The town was a stage stop in the 1870s; visitors often stayed to see the springs or take mineral baths. Construction on the Jackson House began in 1876, and it opened in 1878. The town incorporated in 1880. Poncha Springs is one of the few towns whose primary landowners believed in prohibition. This resulted in a ban on the sale of liquor on any property they owned, thus reducing the ratio of saloons to other businesses. Poncha Springs also had a library, the first in Chaffee County, rare by mining town standards.

Before the 1880s, Poncha Springs was an established health resort, with some one hundred springs whose temperatures varied from 90 to 185 degrees. When the railroad came in 1881, the population grew to over two thousand. Another hotel was built to accommodate all the visitors. The Poncha Springs Hotel competed for a time with the Jackson House, which has hosted some famous guests, including Baby Doe Tabor and Jesse James. But fire struck the town in 1882, destroying most of the frame buildings, including seventeen saloons. The old town was never rebuilt. A few historic buildings remain, including the Jackson Hotel and an early brick schoolhouse.

Poncha Springs Hotel burned down in 1893. Another hotel was built on-site, but it, too, burned in 1903. When the Holman family came in 1904 to manage the springs, they found a large round swimming pool made of rock and completely plastered by hand. Two cabins, two baths and a sleeping room also remained. The springs bubbled out of the mountainside, some of them hot enough to fry an egg. The waters contained large quantities of soda, iron, magnesium, borax, sulfur and arsenic.

In 1935, the City of Salida had the WPA pipe the spring waters into the Salida pool. All the springs were then capped with cement, and the famous Poncha hot springs have been the property of Salida ever since. Today, the water from Poncha Springs is still piped into Salida's Hot Springs Aquatic Center.

A round, sawn-board shelter covers the hot springs in front of the Poncha Springs Hotel. There were approximately fifteen springs with temperatures of 160 degrees Fahrenheit. The waters could boil an egg in less than eight minutes. Photo circa 1900.

JACKSON HOUSE: Built sometime between 1876 and 1878 by Henry A. Jackson, this hotel is still standing and was still in operation until recently. The restored historic building is apparently up for sale.

PONCHA SPRINGS HOTEL: This hotel was built in 1900 and burned down in 1903.

St. Elmo: Ghost Town

Founded in 1880 as a mining town called Forest City, St. Elmo was renamed by Griffith Evans, a founding father, who was reading a book by the same name written by Augusta Evans. St. Elmo, which had drawn the businesses away from Alpine when the railroad came in, was once an important stop for train excursionists on the South Park Line. Tailor-made clothing, oysters and fresh fruit from distant points were easily obtained in St. Elmo. Its decline began in the early 1920s, when the mines shut down and the train discontinued service. With the death of the postmaster in 1952, mail service was curtailed.

The town is listed on the National Register of Historic Places as St. Elmo Historic District, and though still inhabited by a few citizens, it is one of the state's best-preserved ghost towns.

Home Comfort Hotel and Stark Brothers Mercantile Company, circa 1980s.

HOME COMFORT HOTEL: This hotel was built sometime in the 1880s by J.E. McClure and H.C. Bostwick on West Main Street.

In 1881, Anton Stark, a cattleman, became so impressed with St. Elmo that he brought his family to reside there. He had purchased the store and hotel property by 1902. Stark became a boss for one of the local mines, while his wife, Anna, ran the general store and hotel.

The hotel took the top floor of the two-story frame structure, while the downstairs was occupied by Stark Brothers Mercantile. The building was added to in stages and was reported to have the cleanest rooms in town, the best meals and more plentiful supplies than its competition. Of course, there are indications that this opinion may not have been universal.

Salida

Salida, at an elevation of 7,050 feet and surrounded by mountains, is known as the "Jewel of the Arkansas." Founded in 1880, Salida was a significant link in the Denver and Rio Grande Railroad. Its present economy depends strongly on tourism: skiing, rafting, kayaking and outfitting, especially on the Arkansas River.

Salida Hot Springs Aquatic Center is a year-round facility, whose water is piped in several miles from the source in Poncha Springs. The clear, odorless water, once visited by the Ute Indians, flows continually into Salida's pools, warming them naturally. This 1937 WPA project represents Colorado's largest indoor hot springs pool, employing two hundred men to construct the pipeline and buildings. The facility and water line have been updated several times over the years.

BON TON HOTEL: Built before 1904, this hotel's new operators were Mr. and Mrs. Cope in 1904.

THE ELK HOTEL: This hotel was built before 1904.

THE EUROPEAN HOTEL: This hotel was built before 1903 on the banks of the Arkansas River.

HOTEL MONTE CRISTO: Built about 1883 on the tracks of the Denver and Rio Grande Railroad, this hotel was torn down after World War II. The introduction of Pullman sleepers and dining cars ended the demand for overnight rooms and restaurant stops, signaling the end for this railroad hotel.

MAC MORAN HOTEL: This hotel was built before 1900.

MANHATTAN HOTEL: Built in 1901 at 228 North F Street, this hotel remained in operation into the 1930s. It is now listed on the National Register of Historic Places.

MILDRED HOUSE: Built before 1900, this hotel advertised "The Mildred European Plan."

ST. CLAIR HOTEL: Built sometime between 1890 and 1900, this four-story brick structure with a corner tower was operated by C.G. Vaughn in 1904.

WELLSVILLE SPRINGS: Built before 1904, this hotel was operated by V.C. Davenport in 1904.

Turret: Ghost Town

The first settlers in the area cut down wood to make into charcoal. Then came the miners, who found gold, silver and copper. When the Denver and Rio Grande Railroad built a line up the steep grade to Turret in 1881, the miners cheered. Unfortunately, a flood in 1901 wiped out the line, which was never replaced. Although the mines were still producing, the expected "Big Strike" in Turret never came to pass, and the loss of the railroad made it too expensive to ship out the medium-grade ore.

After struggling through many trials, Turret became an official ghost town. Following the death of Pete Schlosser, town founder and postmaster,

The Gregory Hotel, the Turret Sample Room and the Turret Hotel, 1902.

the postal service discontinued mail service and declared Turret a ghost town on Schlosser's birthday, November 12, 1939.

Tales have been told about families moving into Turret during the Depression, living in abandoned houses, planting gardens, hunting deer and smelting gold with blowtorches. The gold could be sold to the government for thirty-two dollars per ounce, and Turret was the poor man's salvation until World War II made city jobs available again.

Turret is located north of Salida, owned by two Colorado natives living in Salida. They have established the Turret Townsite Company, LLC, in an effort to share the local history by selling cabin sites in Turret with strict guidelines to preserve the authenticity of the old town.

GREGORY HOTEL: This hotel was built before 1902.
TURRET HOTEL: Built before 1902, this hotel offered a separate Sample Room for salesmen to display their wares.

CONEJOS COUNTY

"Conejos" is the Spanish word for "rabbits," which populate the area.

Antonito

Once part of Mexico, Antonito was founded in 1880 by the Denver and Rio Grande Railroad. Antonito is located two miles from Conejos, site of the oldest church in Colorado. At an elevation of 7,888 feet, located between the Conejos and San Antonio Rivers, the town is home to the historic Cumbres and Toltec Scenic Narrow Gauge Railroad. This railway is the longest and highest narrow gauge still running, through sixty-four miles of rugged terrain along the Colorado/New Mexico border. The area has long been known for trout fishing and horseback riding.

*CONEJOS RIVER GUEST RANCH: 25390 Highway 17, Antonito, CO 81120; (719) 376-2464; conejosranch.com.

Located in the Rio Grande National Forest, the ranch has approximately one mile of river frontage on the famous Conejos River. The historic, rustic guest ranch, famous for its fishing, is now in its second century of operation. Its beautiful surroundings are perfect for hiking, photography, horseback

The original Conejos River Guest Ranch log house, circa 1930s. The original main house still survives and has been substantially added to over the years.

riding, hunting and snowmobiling in season. Guest horses are also welcome. The ranch has its own menagerie and a stocked pond for children to fish. Its restaurant, the Canyon Café, offers a wide variety of deliciously prepared hearty meals.

The original log lodge, still in use, has been expanded as the property changed hands over the years, and today cabins are also available. Present owners are Leonard and Kathy Nalls, and the ranch foreman is Ms. Shorty Fry.

DEPOT HOTEL & RESTAURANT: This hotel was built sometime before the 1880s and faced the railroad tracks.

GERMANIA HOTEL: This hotel was built before 1904.

PALACE HOTEL: Built before 1904 at 429 Main Street, this hotel is listed on the National Register of Historic Places.

La Jara

The town of La Jara, named for a local creek, is located in the central San Luis Valley. Its mostly Hispanic population descends from settlers who came to the area in the early 1850s to settle on the Sangre de Cristo and Conejos Land Grants. It is still primarily a ranching and farming area.

BLAKE HOTEL: This hotel was built before 1904.

GRANDE HOTEL: Built before 1904, this hotel was operated by Mrs. L. Seyfer in 1904.

ORMOND HOTEL: Built before 1904, this hotel was operated by Mrs. E.A. Brown in 1904.

Platoro

Platoro, at ninety-nine hundred feet in elevation, is in the Rio Grande National Forest, surrounded by the San Juan Wilderness. The town's name was derived from the two Spanish words "plata" and "oro" (silver and gold), and it was founded in the 1880s as a mining town. By 1882, the serious lack of transportation began to adversely affect the town. Although the mines were still productive, the town was too isolated to prosper.

Platoro was also plagued by repeated flooding of the Conejos River. In recent years, a dam was built to create the highest man-made reservoir in North America, the Platoro Reservoir at 10,034 feet, two miles above the town. Today, Platoro has become a quiet resort community, dedicated to fishing.

A dogsled team in front of the Platoro Hotel, 1890–1900.

PLATORO HOTEL: This hotel was built before 1900.

EAGLE COUNTY

This county was created by the Colorado legislature in 1883 from portions of Summit County and named after the Eagle River, which runs through the area. The county seat was originally Red Cliff but moved to the town of Eagle in 1921. Once dependent on mining and agriculture, today's driving force of the area's economy is tourism.

Gypsum

Gypsum was founded in 1881, named for the mineral mined in the area. It is home to an American Gypsum drywall plant and mine. Gypsum is a common mineral associated with sedimentary rock, used in plaster and drywall manufacturing. In the spring of 1905, Theodore Roosevelt spent two weeks hunting in the area; his small party of men killed ten bears and two bobcats on Divide Creek. When the governor of Colorado offered Roosevelt a special permit to kill deer and elk, it was reported that Roosevelt declined, stating that he did not wish to violate Colorado's game laws.

GYPSUM HOTEL: Built by 1903, this hotel was operated by Mrs. J.S. Strauss in 1904.

SWEETWATER HOTEL: Built before 1904, this hotel was operated by Mrs. N. Davenport in 1904.

TRAVELERS HOTEL: Built before 1904, this hotel was operated by Mrs. W.J. Sherman in 1904.

ULIN HOTEL: This hotel was built before 1903.

Holy Cross City: Ghost Town

The Mount of the Holy Cross is the northernmost fourteen-thousand-foot peak in the Sawatch Range of the Rockies. It is located in the Holy Cross Wilderness, near the ghost town of Holy Cross City. The cross formation can only be seen from the summit of Notch Mountain, which stands immediately east of the Mount of the Holy Cross. The mountain was

The Timberline Hotel, circa 1880–90.

discovered in 1869 and progressively gained notoriety. Organized Christian pilgrimages to the mountain began in the 1920s, and by the 1930s, they were drawing thousands of participants. Once declared a National Monument, the mountain lost this status in 1950, when the cross formation lost much of its definition due to rockslides and erosion.

The town was named for the distinctive cross-shaped snowfield on the mountain's northeast face. A few cabins and abandoned mining equipment are all that remain of Holy Cross City. The first mines were staked in 1880, and their ore appeared to promise a boom. But the deeper the miners dug, the less valuable the ore became. At its peak, the town's population was about three hundred, but most of the mines were abandoned by 1886.

TIMBERLINE HOTEL: This hotel was built sometime in the 1880s.

McCoy

This area is known for its fossil beds. Conifer fossils found at McCoy are some of the earliest known in North America. Other fossilized plant life and creatures discovered here include snails, crinoids, corals and shark remains.

MCCOY HOTEL: Built before 1904, this hotel was operated by C.H. McCoy in 1904.

Minturn

Minturn was settled at the confluence of Gore Creek and the Eagle River in the late 1800s. Early residents were homesteaders, but others mined silver in the mountains above town. When the Denver and Rio Grande Railroad arrived in 1887, Minturn changed from a quiet community to a busy railroad and mining town. The development of Vail Resort in the 1960s prevented the town's economic downturn, usually following collapse of the mining industry. Minturn, more fortunate than many mining towns, is today a thriving mountain community.

AMERICAN HOUSE: This hotel was built before 1904.
D. & R.G. HOTEL: Built before 1904, this hotel was operated by the Denver and Rio Grande Railroad in 1904.

Red Cliff

Red Cliff, 8,650 feet in elevation, was founded in 1879 and named for red quartzite cliffs in the area. There has been a settlement at the junction of the Turkey Creek and Eagle River ever since the Rohm party set up permanent camp there in 1879, making it the oldest town in Eagle County. By 1900, Red Cliff was a lively mining town with saloons, a bank, sawmills and an opera house.

The town's first hotel was the Star, a two-story building with cloth partitions and a surprising reputation as the most luxurious lodging in Red Cliff until the Quartzite Hotel was built some years later. In 1882, the following hotels, in addition to the Star and Quartzite, were operating: Southern Hotel, Pacific Hotel, Mountain House and Iowa House.

Like many towns of the period, Red Cliff suffered from disastrous fires. In 1882, fire burned down the Southern Hotel and then spread along Water Street, wreaking havoc in that part of the town. Two more fires prompted citizens to establish a water system in 1887.

Town fathers were determined that Red Cliff would be a proper town. The bodies of two men who had shot and killed each other in a gunfight were refused burial in the town's new cemetery, as it was thought that allowing murderers to be the first customers would give the new cemetery a bad name. As a compromise, the two bodies were buried beside the road to the graveyard.

In 1881, the Denver and Rio Grande reached Red Cliff and opened for freight and passenger service, with overnight Pullman Sleepers available. Red Cliff's surrounding area offers beautiful scenery, including views of the Mount of the Holy Cross.

EAGLE HOTEL: Built before 1904, this hotel was operated by William Greiner in 1904.

IOWA HOUSE: No information available.

THE MOUNTAIN HOUSE: No information available.

PACIFIC HOTEL: No information available.

QUARTZITE HOTEL: Built before 1904, this hotel was operated by George Jones in 1904.

SOUTHERN HOTEL: Built prior to 1882, the Southern burned down in 1882.

STAR HOTEL: No information available.

Wolcott

Once known as Russell, Wolcott was an important rail shipping point for agricultural products. The town was renamed for Colorado senator Edward Oliver Wolcott.

In 1886, a wagon road was completed to Steamboat Springs, and the subsequent arrival of the railroad in 1887 made Wolcott one of the largest shipping points on the Western Slope. At the height of activity, two thousand cars of cattle were shipped from Wolcott yearly, and the community catered to travelers and those involved with cattle transport. The town boasted livery barns, stockyards, a hotel, a general store, a saloon and a blacksmith shop. Wolcott's prosperity came to a sudden end with the opening of the Moffat Tunnel in 1928, which caused rail traffic to bypass the once prosperous community.

HOTEL HAWLEY: Built before 1904, this hotel was operated by L.S. Hawley in 1904.
WOLCOTT HOTEL: Built before 1904, this hotel was operated by H.E. Asmus in 1904.
MCCOY'S HOTEL: Built before 1904, this hotel was operated by C.H. McCoy in 1904.

GRAND COUNTY

Grand County takes its name from the Grand River, an early name for the Colorado River. It was created out of Summit County in 1874. Prior to the construction of the Granby/Grand County Airport, U.S. Highway 40 over Berthoud Pass and Amtrak rail service, this alpine-like region was mostly inaccessible. But the area is today popular for hiking, biking, golfing, skiing, fly-fishing and just about any other outdoor sport one might wish for.

Grand County owes much of its pristine qualities to the U.S. government and the State of Colorado, which own 68 percent of its land. As a result, the local four-legged wildlife can expect to continue roaming the county from Rocky Mountain National Park in the north to Winter Park in the south, with little intervention from the two-leggeds.

Berthoud Pass

This pass is located on the line between Clear Creek and Grand Counties and was named for Edward L. Berthoud, chief surveyor of the Colorado

A postcard of the Berthoud Pass Inn, circa 1925.

Central Railroad in the 1870s. Berthoud, along with famed mountain man Jim Bridger, discovered the pass in July 1861, while surveying a route for the railroad. Berthoud reported the pass as suitable for a wagon road but not a railroad, and so it is driven over today via U.S. Highway 40.

BERTHOUD PASS INN: In operation from 1915 to 1939, at an elevation of 11,306 feet, this log inn stood at the summit of the pass. It was built by Charles Fitchett, who helped to survey the old Berthoud Pass wagon road when plans were made to change it into a highway. The inn was built for summer tourists to buy snacks and souvenirs, although skiers used it during winter months as well. The building was struck by lightning and dismantled in 1939.

HOTEL EVANS SPRUCE LODGE: This hotel was built about 1900 on the west slope of Berthoud Pass.

Corona: Only a Memory

This tiny settlement at the apex of Rollins Pass, at 11,660 feet in elevation, was built in 1904 for the Denver and Salt Lake Railroad. The town served as a shelter for the engine crews and consisted of a café, a telegraph office, a small hotel and a few shops—the entire unusual settlement was constructed under snow sheds. A brick, single-story hotel was built for tourists who came via rail from Denver. The summit winds were so severe that it was often necessary to cable down the brick hotel, lest it be blown away. In

A postcard of the Corona Hotel, circa 1918: "Highest hotel in the world, elev. 11,794 ft., Denver and Salt Lake R.R."

1928, a tunnel was finished beneath the pass, making the railroad over it unnecessary. Corona and its hotel were dismantled and burned by the U.S. Forestry Service. Today, nothing remains of Corona but its ghosts.

CORONA HOTEL: Built about 1905, this hotel was razed in 1928.

Fraser

Set in Middle Park in the Fraser River Valley at 8,550 feet, Fraser was established in 1904 for the Moffat Railroad. Fraser, Colorado, and International Falls, Michigan, vie for title of "Icebox of the Nation." Fraser's annual mean temperature of 32.5 degrees Fahrenheit makes it the coldest incorporated town in the continental United States.

GASKILL'S: Built before 1904, this hotel was operated by L.D. Gaskill in 1904.

Grand Lake

Formed by glaciers, Grand Lake is Colorado's largest and deepest natural lake, dropping to 265 feet. Located on the border of the Rocky Mountain National Park, Grand Lake is the headwaters of the "Grand River," now known as the Colorado River. The lake is fed by high mountain runoff; its waters are clear and pristine. Grand Lake has welcomed visitors since the Rocky Mountain National Park's opening in 1915.

European hunting parties first discovered Grand Lake in the 1850s, building lodges and hiring local mountain men as guides. By 1867, the area was permanently settled. The town of Grand Lake was officially established in 1881. Its first residents were miners and hunting guides. In the late 1870s, silver was discovered near Grand Lake, bringing more prospectors into the mountain community.

Trail Ridge Road, usually open from late May to mid-October, reaches 12,183 feet at its peak elevation and connects Grand Lake to Estes Park. As soon as the road opened, Grand Lake transformed into a bustling town, bringing the usual strife. Political differences over location of the county seat led to a bloody Fourth of July shootout. But despite violence and the eventual waning economy, some miners permanently settled the area, while other visitors returned yearly. To accommodate guests, a number of small hotels were constructed, and local Lodgepole pine was the building material of choice.

This gave rise to a unique form of architecture still apparent in Grand Lake today—a rustic form of Victorian architecture identified by log construction and steam-bent saplings. It has been called Victorian Gothic and Adirondack Rustic. Many of Grand Lake's historic buildings are still in use.

The Adams Hotel, circa 1900.

ADAMS HOTEL: Built about 1890, this hotel was destroyed by fire in 1903.

HOTEL BELLEVUE: Built before 1904, this hotel was operated by P.H. Smith in 1904.

KAUFMAN HOTEL: Built before 1904, this hotel was operated by Mrs. J.L. Adams in 1904.

RUSTIC HOTEL: This hotel was built in 1900 on the west shore of Grand Lake by Christian F. Young and his wife, Josephine, who later remarried and became Mrs. H.C. Langley.

THROCKMORTON VILLA: Built before 1904, this hotel was operated by Mrs. E.J. Throckmorton in 1904.

*HOT SULPHUR SPRINGS: Hot Sulphur Springs in Grand County is the site of one of Colorado's many hot springs. Seven natural springs have been flowing constantly for hundreds of years, surfacing at around 104 to 126 degrees Fahrenheit. Over 200,000 gallons of natural, hot, mineral-rich water flow through twenty-two pools and baths every day at controlled temperatures of 95 to 112 degrees. These mineral springs were once used by the Ute Indians, who believed the waters possessed healing properties. The springs fell into disrepair but were reopened in recent years and blessed by a Ute elder. The springs are now known as the Hot Sulphur Springs Resort (5609 County Road 20, Hot Sulphur Springs, CO 80451; 970-725-3306).

KINNEY HOUSE: Built before 1886, this hotel was operated by Mrs. L.E. Farley in 1904.

McQUEARY HOUSE: Built before 1904, this hotel was operated by Mrs. M. McQueary in 1904.

MIDDLE PARK HOTEL: This hotel was built before 1886.

RIVERSIDE HOTEL: 509 Grand Avenue, Hot Sulphur Springs, CO 80451. Built in 1903, the Historic Riverside, renovated in 2008, still possesses authentic turn-of-the-century charm. It has fourteen guest rooms and a restaurant overlooking the river. Located on the banks of the Colorado River, the hotel is currently for sale.

THE WILLOWS: Built before 1904, this hotel was operated by Frank Byers in 1904.

A pool at Hot Sulphur Springs, 1912.

GUNNISON COUNTY

Gunnison County is named for John W. Gunnison, U.S. Army officer and captain in the Army Topographical Engineers, who surveyed for the transcontinental railroad in 1853.

Cebolla Hot Springs

Cebolla Hot Springs are now under the Blue Mesa Reservoir, all inundated. Three historic towns on the Gunnison River were abandoned and flooded, or moved, in the 1960s, when Blue Mesa Reservoir was created. These famous fishing places were Iola, Cebolla and Sapinero.

Lost in the flood were the following hotels:

GOLD COIN HOTEL: This hotel was built before 1904.
IOLA HOTEL: Built before 1904, this hotel was operated by C.A. Green in 1904.
SPENCER HOTEL: Built before 1904, this hotel was operated by Mrs. Campbell in 1904.
SPORTSMEN'S HOTEL: Built before 1904, this hotel was ooperated by J.J. Carpenter in 1904.
VULCAN HOTEL: Built before 1904, this hotel was operated by J.A. Weirs in 1904.

Crested Butte

The first white men to explore the East River Valley were trappers and surveyors, Captain John Gunnison among them. The county bears his name. Once a summer location of the Ute tribe prior to white intrusion, Crested Butte soon became a coal and silver mining town and more recently has become known for skiing, biking and other winter sports, with the construction of a ski area in the 1960s.

The town is listed on the National Register of Historic Places for its Victorian architecture. One singular contribution to sanitation has become a tourist attraction of sorts. Crested Butte's two-story outhouse, built in the 1800s, is still standing. Some years, the snow was so deep that it buried the outhouses, so a clever, unknown Colorado carpenter designed the two-story model, which can reportedly be seen today in an alley behind the Company Store.

ELK MOUNTAIN HOUSE: Built in 1881 on the corner of Elk and Fourth Streets, this hotel was operated by C.J. Del in 1904. The large frame hotel faced the Elk Mountains and was heated by several wood stoves, which eventually caused its top floors to catch fire. The salvaged lower portion was added to and became the Mexican restaurant Donita's Cantina (970-349-6674).

Gunnison

This town, like the county, was named in honor of John W. Gunnison, surveyor for the transcontinental railroad in 1853. After the Utes were forced out, the white population moved in. Initially a ranching and mining town, it became a trade center for smaller communities in the area and is now a tourist destination.

Gunnison became the official county seat in 1877. In 1880, the railroad arrived, bringing hopes for prosperity. But by 1883, a bust had taken place and half the population left. Ore mined in the area was not as rich as its reputation, resulting in another mining town's economy biting the dust.

But the Taylor River, Tomichi and Cebolla Creeks have long been known as some of the best trout fishing spots in the Rockies. With the opening of Crested Butte Ski Area in 1963, Gunnison has become a favorite tourist destination.

DAWSON HOUSE: This hotel was built before 1883.
JOINTED ROD RESORT: This hotel was built before 1904 and was operated by A.L. Wilson in 1904.

A postcard of the La Veta Hotel, Gunnison, Colorado.

A humorous postcard advertising free meals at the La Veta Hotel and Gunnison's weather, 1914.

LA VETA HOTEL: This hotel was in operation from 1884–85 to 1944 at 219 South Boulevard. It was one of the grandest buildings in Gunnison. It hosted passenger depot facilities for the Denver and Rio Grande Railroad and featured a four-story center, with a mansard roof and dormers, open walkways with iron railings, second- and third-story balconies, two three-story wings, stone window lintels and first-floor storefronts. The finest materials were used in its construction; its black walnut, oak and ash stairway rose to a forty- by sixty-foot rotunda that supported a skylight.

In 1912, as a promotion, the hotel began offering free meals to guests on any day the sun refused to shine in Gunnison and kept a record of meals it had given away beneath the lobby clock. In thirty years, the hotel gave away only twenty meals.

But the town's interest in large and impressive structures was over. Local organizations tried to rescue the hotel in the 1940s but failed, and the building sold at a sheriff's auction for $8,350 in 1944. It was soon after reduced to a one-story structure; its valuable timber was salvaged.

THE MARSTON: This hotel was built before 1904 and operated by Vernon Davis in 1904.

PALISADES HOTEL: Built before 1882 on Main Street, this hotel burned down in 1905. It was a stone, two-story structure on a prominent corner.

Irwin: Ghost Town

Irwin was founded in 1880 near Crested Butte, following the discovery of silver in 1879. The population grew to one thousand within six months. But with the demonetizing of silver in 1884, the town's economy

The Hotel Belmont in Irwin (Ruby Camp), 1882.

collapsed, and many of its buildings were dismantled and taken to other mining towns in the 1890s.

All that remains are a few foundations and the town cemetery.

HOTEL BELMONT: Built prior to 1882, this frame building was a two-story, flat-roofed Italianate with brackets under the eaves, three second-story arched windows in front and six windows over the store on the side.

Sapinero

Sapinero was relocated to the shore of the Blue Mesa Reservoir after its original site, a mile away, was inundated in 1963.

RAINBOW HOTEL: Built in 1908 by H.S. Carpenter, this fishing resort was torn down in 1962 for the Blue Mesa Reservoir. The hotel now sleeps with the fishes.

SAPINERO RESORT HOTEL AND MERCANTILE COMPANY: Built about 1910, this resort was razed for the Blue Mesa Reservoir in 1962.

HINSDALE COUNTY

Hinsdale County was formed in 1874 from Conejos County, named for early pioneer and lieutenant governor of Colorado George Hinsdale. The least populated county in the state, located in southwest central Colorado, its county seat is Lake City.

Lake City

Set in the heart of the San Juan Mountain Range, minutes from San Cristobal Lake, Lake City's climate just escapes classification as semi-arid. Extreme daily temperature swings are common.

Explorers first discovered gold in 1848 in the valley, but fear of Chief Ouray's Utes kept prospectors and miners away until 1874, when the Bunot Treaty opened the area to whites. The Denver and Rio Grande Railroad's arrival in 1889 brought affordable transportation for ore, and the mines swung into full operation. Until the silver bust, Lake City had two banks, two breweries, seven saloons, a newspaper and the first church on the Western Slope. Lake City's most productive years were 1876 and 1877, when the population swelled to twenty-five hundred.

Back in "the day," Lake City had a neighborhood known as Hell's Acre, brimming with thieves, drunks, con artists and murderers. When two reprobates who ran a sleazy dance hall killed the Lake City sheriff, incensed residents broke the thugs out of jail and strung them up on a nearby bridge. The killers' fate was roundly approved by most of the town, the paper reported.

In 1874, Alferd Packer, Lake City's infamous cannibal, was jailed for eating five prospectors when the group became trapped in a blizzard on nearby Slumgullion Pass. He was tried for murder in 1883 at the Hinsdale County Courthouse. Packer represented himself and was duly convicted. He spent some time in the Colorado Territorial Prison in Cañon City but was released on a technicality. Afterward, he allegedly became a vegetarian and made a simple living selling autographed pictures of himself, a better career choice than that of lawyer.

Today, Lake City is an excellent example of well-preserved, turn-of-the-century architecture, maintaining over seventy-five buildings from the 1800s in one of Colorado's largest historical districts.

LA VETA HOUSE: This hotel was operated by G.B. Whitman in 1904.
OCCIDENTAL HOUSE: This hotel was operated by D.T. McLeod in 1904.
PUEBLO HOUSE: This hotel was operated by J.T. Allison in 1904.

Jackson County

Jackson County, thought to have been named for President Andrew Jackson (for some incalculable reason), is located in the high basin known as North Park. The term "park" comes from the French word for game preserve, as North Park was once filled with herds of deer, antelope and buffalo. There were so many buffalo that the Utes, believing the surrounding mountains held the game herds in the valley, called the area "Bull Pen." In 1861, Colorado formed seventeen counties, including Larimer, part of which would, in 1909, become Jackson County.

Initially, whites avoided North Park, which was Ute and Arapahoe hunting grounds, so strongly defended that white settlers feared venturing in. But when valuable minerals were discovered in North Park, Grand County claimed it as part of its county, as did Larimer, and it was contested all the way to the state Supreme Court. In 1886, the court decided for Larimer, making the North Park residents unhappy until Jackson County's formation.

Walden

This town, named for early settler Marcus Walden, is the Jackson County seat. It is built on a high plain at the headwaters of the North Platte River.

WOODS HOTEL: This hotel was built before 1895.

An eclectic gathering of townspeople, one dog and a burro in front of Woods Hotel, 1895.

LAKE COUNTY

Lake County, named for local Twin Lakes, is the highest county in the United States, bounded on all sides by fourteen-thousand-foot peaks. The two highest mountains in Colorado—Mount Elbert and Mount Massive—form its western boundary and are visible from most of the county.

Leadville

Leadville is the Lake County seat and its only municipality. Its history began in 1860 with the discovery of gold south of town. Some eight thousand prospectors flooded into "Oro City," as they called their rough town of tents and cabins. During the next five years, more than $4 million in gold was discovered using sluice and pan—more than any other Colorado site. Within five years, the gold was gone. Next came the silver boom. Leadville became one of the raunchiest mining towns in the Rockies.

By 1880, the town had over thirty thousand residents; innumerable stores, hotels and boardinghouses; and over one hundred saloons, dance halls, gambling joints and brothels. Soon, the Colorado and Southern High Line, a narrow gauge railroad, was serving the mineral belt.

Horace A.W. Tabor, who owned a local mercantile store with his wife, Augusta, speculated in mining and made millions from silver. He built Leadville an opera house in 1879, followed by the Bank of Leadville and the Tabor Grand Hotel. He also left his wife to wed the divorced, beautiful and much younger Elizabeth McCourt "Baby" Doe. While society snubbed her, Tabor became an important political figure.

Leadville also gave opportunity to other financial careers, the Guggenheims, Marshall Fields and W.B. Daniels among them. Doc Holliday's time in Leadville was less laudable. While there are conflicting accounts, records indicate that he shot one Bill Allen in 1884. Holliday was released on bail of $8,000, raised by friends, and in 1885, he was acquitted. Allen, who did not die, had the dubious honor of being the last man shot by Holliday.

In 1893, the repeal of the Silver Purchase Act ruined Tabor and many others. Baby Doe froze to death at Leadville's Matchless Mine. Silver was over, but mining for zinc, lead and copper continued. Mining's last great hurrah took place in 1918, when the Climax Molybdenum Mine opened north of Leadville, employing over three thousand workers and supplying half the world's molybdenum.

In 1889, Congress established a National Fish Hatchery on the east side of Mount Massive, which is today the oldest fish hatchery west of the

Mississippi River. Seventy square blocks of Leadville have been designated as a National Historic Landmark of Victorian architecture, featuring over fifty nineteenth-century buildings. Other local attractions include the historic mining district, the railroad, more museums than any town in Colorado and, at 10,152 feet above sea level, the world's highest microbrewery.

CLARENDON HOTEL: This hotel was built before 1881.

*DELAWARE HOTEL: 700 Harrison Avenue, Leadville, CO 80461; 719-486-1418, 800-748-2004; delawarehotel.com.

Completed in 1886 by the Callaway brothers, the Delaware was designed by British architect George King and named for the Callaways' home state. The Callaways started with mercantile stores, and as they prospered, they built the Callaway Block, housing the hotel, first-floor businesses and offices. This was a very forward-thinking plan for its day.

John Callaway was the first proprietor, described as a dapper man with wire-rimmed glasses, a derby and a vested suit who played classical music on a phonograph.

Notables of the day such as Butch Cassidy, John Phillip Sousa and Unsinkable Molly Brown frequented Leadville, in all likelihood stopping at the Delaware. Doc Holliday also stayed at the hotel, preferring a particular second-floor room with a view of Main Street, as he could check the street out front and make a quick getaway, if needed, by jumping out a window onto an adjoining roof and running down the back alley. During one stay, some testy business involving a gun and a bartender cut short that particular visit.

Even Leadville's tragic heroine, Baby Doe Tabor, feet wrapped in gunnysacks, often came to the hotel's second-floor office to write letters and warm herself, frequently staying most of the day.

The Delaware was extensively renovated in 1992, resulting in thirty-six handsome rooms on both second and third floors, furnished in antiques. Its ground floor features an antique shop, a bar in the lobby and Callaway's Restaurant, a Victorian bistro offering favorite western dishes and an eclectic menu of signature soups, salads (such as pear-walnut and cranberry coleslaw) and a special Victorian sampler plate. Buffalo chili is a local favorite, as are home-smoked barbecued ribs, brisket and chicken flavored by Callaway's secret sauce. Callaway's also offers traditional Sunday afternoon tea, but for those not partial to cucumber sandwiches, Cowboy Tea and Sweet Tooth Tea are tasty variations of Leadville-style fare. Dinners are served Fridays and Saturdays, June through September.

The Delaware Hotel today is Leadville's Crown Jewel. *Photo courtesy of the Delaware Hotel.*

The Delaware, known as the "Crown Jewel of Leadville," filled with history and antiques of the era, is still going strong. In 2011, it will celebrate its 125th anniversary with continuing exhibits, presentations, reenactments, a Victorian fashion show and special events highlighting Leadville's surprisingly varied cultural ethnicity.

GRAND HOTEL: This hotel was built before 1879 on Chestnut Street.

PALACE HOTEL: This hotel was built before 1879 on State Street (later named Second Street).

TABOR GRAND HOTEL: The Tabor Grand was opened in 1885 at Seventh and Harrison Streets across the street from the Delaware Hotel. George King was the architect.

When the Leadville Hotel Company came up short-funded for plans to build a first-class hotel, local silver baron H.A.W. Tabor supplied the money, and the hotel subsequently bore his name. The four-story hotel had 117 rooms, steam heat, a formal dining room and a wine cellar. Extravagance was the byword, evidenced by the hotel's lobby floor, which was inlaid with silver dollars.

The Kitchen Brothers acquired the hotel in 1887 and renamed it, not so surprisingly but rather distractingly, the Kitchen Hotel. But the brothers knew more than how to run its kitchen, and the hotel flourished for a while, hosting dignitaries and celebrities. At the height of its success, in 1891, the Kitchens sold to an investment company, which renamed their establishment the Hotel Vendome.

Two years later, the silver crash decimated local economy. Nevertheless, the Vendome struggled into the twentieth century, repeatedly changing hands like a square dancer, never closing. While the hotel still stands and has once again been named the Tabor Grande Hotel, it is now apartments.

HOTEL VENDOME: Originally the Tabor Grand Hotel (see above), this hotel was renamed twice by 1890. It was still operating in 1931.

HOTEL WINDSOR: This hotel was built sometime in the 1880s.

Twin Lakes

Twin Lakes adjoins two lakes at the foot of Colorado's highest peak, Mount Elbert. The town was once a transportation hub for mining towns but has evolved into a beautiful place for recreation.

HOTEL CAMPION: This hotel was originally built in 1895 by John Francis Campion as his family's "Country Villa." Campion was president of Napite Mining Co. and vice president of the Denver, Northwest and Pacific Railroad. Upon his death in 1916, the home was turned into a hotel. It was reached via the Colorado Midland Railway and featured an oversized cupola and many windowed gables, with its own power plant beside the lake.

INTER-LAKEN: Built before 1886. It was a frame hotel with "Inter-Laken" painted above the door and antlers adorning the front gable.

MINERAL COUNTY

Mineral County is located in the mountains of southern Colorado. Having 95 percent public lands, it offers a wealth of unspoiled scenic beauty. A number of ghost towns haunt the countryside.

Creede

Creede is located near the headwaters of the Rio Grande River, which flows through the San Juan Mountains and San Luis Valley. The town, named for prospector Nicholas C. Creede, is the only town in Mineral County. At an elevation of eighty-five hundred feet, it was the site of Colorado's last silver boom in the 1800s; at its peak, it had some ten thousand residents. In 1883, the railroad brought the first tourists to Creede, with the opening of the Wagon Wheel Gap depot. Fishermen could ride the railroad to a favorite spot, jump off the train, fish all day and then catch a returning ride back.

Creede was firmly established with the discovery of large deposits of silver in 1892, and the population soared. Simultaneously, a reform movement against gambling clubs and saloons in Denver prompted many owners of the city's major gambling houses to relocate to Creede. One of these shady proprietors was infamous con man, Jefferson Randolph "Soapy" Smith, who opened the Orleans Club and soon dominated Creede's underworld.

Creede also became host to Bat Masterson; Robert Ford, the man who killed outlaw Jesse James; and William Sidney "Cap" Light, Creede's first deputy sheriff and brother-in-law of Soapy Smith.

One of Creede's citizens made a respectable name for himself. Jack Dempsey, famous prizefighter, lived in Creede as a boy. His mother, who operated a local boardinghouse, would eventually be rewarded for her labors by her son's gift of a mansion and serving staff to wait on her.

In 1892, a major fire destroyed most of the business district. Three days later, Edward O'Kelley walked into Robert Ford's tent saloon and shot him dead. The town of Creede was willing to keep in the game, but the anti-gambling movement in Denver was over. Big city saloonkeepers took their trade back to their old neighborhoods, leaving vice business to the locals.

With the Silver Panic of 1893, Creede's bubble burst, along with those of the other mining towns, as the price of silver sank from $1.29 to fifty cents per ounce, and most of the silver mines shut down.

But Creede was one of the few towns to have enough other minerals to stay alive and never became a ghost town, though its population declined significantly. By tenaciously refusing to surrender, Creede has today become a historic mining town devoted to tourism.

*CREEDE HOTEL: 120 North Main Street, Creede, CO 81130; 719-658-2608; creedehotel.com.

The first hotel by this name was built before 1892 and burned down in the town fire. Today's Creede Hotel and Restaurant is located in the former Zang's Hotel building (see Zang's Hotel). The Creede Hotel of this century is a small, charming inn, with four restored guestrooms occupying the historic 1892 building on Main Street. All rooms have private baths; two of the upstairs guestrooms share the front balcony.

During the 1900s, Zang's Hotel, once considered the best in town, declined to the point of being categorized as "extremely rustic." But its bar downstairs was a popular hangout for miners, drifters and, of course, politicians. The list of its patrons is long, including western icon John Wayne.

Since its reincarnation as today's Creede Hotel and Restaurant, the old Zang's has redeemed its shady reputation, having undergone much interior renovation, while its original exterior remains much the same as it was a century ago. Today's Creede Hotel, filled with history and more than a few secrets, is a wonderful place to rediscover the authentic flavor of Colorado mountain life in the late 1800s. There have been reports that a few old boarders may still be around; guests have heard and seen strange things in the night. Bring along your favorite ghost hunter.

The Creede Hotel, located in the former Zang's Hotel building.

The Creede Hotel and Restaurant offers elegant dinners featuring hand-cut steaks, fish flown in overnight from Honolulu, ever-changing pasta dishes, local game entrees and much more. The exceptional food is enhanced with good wines, a pleasant atmosphere and friendly hospitality. During the summer season, guests can choose to dine in the hotel's main dining room or among flowers and shimmering aspen on the porch or patio.

ZANG'S HOTEL: This hotel was built about 1892 by John Zang, a Denver brewer of beer and its proprietor. At one time, there were close to one hundred such "hotels" in Creede. Zang's Hotel, whose humble owner named it for himself, was considered one of the town's best. When the first Zang's burned down in Creede's 1906 fire, it was hurriedly rebuilt and soon in operation again. Of all the hastily knocked together buildings in early Creede, Zang's Hotel, of basic but sturdy frame construction, was considered the fanciest place to stay.

Its five upstairs rooms, and at least that many downstairs, housed miners, drummers and others whose professions were less easily defined. Zang's famous (or infamous) boarders included con artist town boss Soapy Smith, Poker Alice Tubbs and Calamity Jane, whose pictures upstairs in the hotel will terminate any attempts to glamorize them. Bob Ford, baby-faced assassin of Jessie James, also tucked in at the old Zang's, prior to his own assassination.

Early photos show the stone building in back of Zang's Hotel as a family-type dwelling, with a barnyard or court between the two. At some point, the stone home was converted into an apartment for the madam and the cribs, where her girls conducted business. Chorus girls from the opera house next door, which is now the Creede Repertory Theatre, used the cribs for costume changes. As the law began to crack down on prostitution, later owners turned these back rooms into legitimate rentals.

Nevertheless, and despite this minor affront to morality, John Zang and his wife ran a good business and were well respected in the community. Go figure.

Unfortunately, Zang did not meet an inspiring end. In 1891, a local paper gave the account that Zang had invaded the home of a woman whose husband was away. It stated that Mrs. Michael LeFevre, her clothing shredded, was discovered with the traditional smoking gun—and Zang's dead body, shot in the face, on her floor. It seems Zang, fifty-five, had attempted to force his attentions on her, and she had struggled with him, broken away, grabbed her husband's revolver and fled. When Zang continued pursuit, she shot him at close range, instantly killing him. Mrs. LeFevre, in her ruined garb, was found calmly washing dishes in the kitchen. That was her story, and she was sticking to it. Zang's side of the gory drama will never be told, as he wasn't talking.

Showing much emotion at the coroner's inquest, LeFevre claimed that Zang had torn her clothes; had struck her in the face, blackening her eye; and had thrown her on the bed three times—and only then had she grabbed the revolver. Zang chased her to the kitchen, where she ordered him four times to leave, but after his failure to comply, she dispatched him with her old man's .45. The coroner's jury returned a verdict that Mrs. LeFevre had acted in self-defense. In an odd sidebar to the story, the paper reported that Mrs. LeFevre, having regained her composure, would be traveling to Denver with her husband to attend Zang's burial at Riverside.

There is yet a belated clause to the tale. Mrs. Zang, after displaying extravagant grief over the loss of her husband, continued to operate Zang's Hotel until 1919, when she sold out, shortly thereafter remarried and left the area.

Wagon Wheel Gap

The settlement was named for wagon remains found in the area. Settlers, including Kit Carson's brother-in-law, Tom Boggs, farmed the land at Wagon Wheel Gap about 1840. In 1875, a depot was built by the Denver and Rio Grande Railroad for tourists heading to the area's hot springs. By 1870, many had flocked in to take the waters, and as word spread, Wagon Wheel Gap was expected to become the next fashionable resort. But before that happened, the interest in spas diminished, and the area became popular for fishing instead.

THE GAP HOTEL: Built before 1904, this hotel was operated by J.A. Murray in 1904.
HOT SPRINGS HOTEL: Built before 1904, with baths, this hotel was operated by Ellwood Bagley in 1904.

PARK COUNTY

Park County is situated high in the Rockies in the center of the state and is known for its spectacular scenery and recreation.

Bailey

Bailey was named for William Bailey, who settled the area in 1864. Set in the Platte Canyon area, in the Pike National Forest, Bailey has long been

Glen Isle's rare 1878 cast-iron and glass Victorian fish tank. The top tier of the tank is actually a fountain composed of four lions' heads, which drew fresh water through a pipe in the floor and sprayed it into the glass and iron basin below. *Photo courtesy Jill Dean, Glen Isle.*

a refuge from the stress of city life, offering exceptional scenery for camping, hiking and fly-fishing.

ESCANABA HOTEL: This hotel was built before 1904.
FAIRVIEW HOUSE: This hotel was built before 1904.
*GLEN ISLE ON THE PLATTE: PO Box 128, Bailey, CO 80421; 303-838-5461; coloradodirectory.com/glenisleresort.

Built about 1900, this hotel has been owned by the same family since 1923. This timeless, rustic hotel, situated on the North Fork of the beautiful South Platte River, is one of few remaining late Victorian resorts in South Platte Canyon, west of Denver. The main lodge features large timbers and a stone fireplace, and the dining room boasts an original, extraordinary 1875 glass and iron, two-tiered pedestal fish tank, which is also a fountain, and once housed fresh mountain trout for guests. Glen Isle is on the National Register of Historic Places; its lodge is open June through mid-September, and cabins are open all year.

THE KIOWA LODGE: Built sometime between 1900 and 1926 and known as "Hotel Beautiful," Kiowa Lodge in Bailey was one of the many grand hotels along the Denver South Park and Pacific Railway. Unfortunately, few of these railroad hotels remain today.

Shawnee

Located in the Platte Canyon on the North Fork of the South Platte River, the settlement was first known as Fairville, but the name was changed to

The sunroom of the Shawnee Lodge, circa 1905–10.

Shawnee with the building of the Shawnee Lodge. In 1886, James Price from England homesteaded the area, building the Grandview Hotel in 1899. In 1900, in conjunction with the Colorado and Southern Railway, Price built the Shawnee Lodge. Shawnee became a popular fishing resort. The local economy was founded on tourism, ranching, farming, logging and winter jobs at the Maddox Ice Co., which closed in 1937.

GRAND VIEW HOTEL: Built in 1899, this was James Price's first hotel. The versatile property later became a private residence, a store and a cemetery. It was operated by J.W. Price in 1904.

SHAWNEE LODGE: Built in 1900 by James Price, this hotel burned down in 1929. It was operated by E.A. Thayer in 1904.

Como

Como is a historic mining settlement founded during the Pikes Peak gold rush of 1859. In 1879, Como became the site of a roundhouse of the Denver, South Park and Pacific Railroad, which extended over Kenosha Pass to mining areas during Colorado's silver boom. The roundhouse served as a junction for trains going north over Boreas Pass. The town retains many historic buildings, including the roundhouse, in the process of being renovated as a tourist attraction.

CASSELL'S HOTEL: This was a summer resort in the South Platte Canyon, on the Colorado and Southern Railway in Park County, operated by D.N. Cassell.

*COMO DEPOT HOTEL B&B: 17 Sixth Street, Como, CO 80432; 719-836-2594.

Originally called the Pacific Hotel, the first Como Hotel was constructed in 1897 to serve passengers on the Denver, South Park and Pacific Railway from Denver. The present owners operate the property as a bed-and-breakfast and restaurant. The Como Depot Hotel is on the National Historic Register, as is the restaurant, the Como Eating House.

Como, filled with railroad history, was an important center for the Denver, South Park and Pacific Railroad, housing the largest roundhouse on the line, whose stone section still remains. The depot itself was built about 1879. Simultaneously that same year, the Gilman Hotel was built

Cassell's Hotel, viewed across the pond, circa 1910–20.

on the site. When the Denver, Leadville and Gunnison Railroad took over the line in 1882, it enlarged the Gilman into the Pacific Hotel, which burned down in 1896. The current Como Eating House was built in 1897 as a replacement.

Fairplay

Set in the center of the state and surrounded by mountains, this area was called South Park by early traders and trappers. The Pikes Peak gold rush saw a virtual army of miners stream into the county. The mining district, in about 1859, was first called Fairplay Diggings by miners who had been turned away from other established sites, where they had been refused a claim. The term "Fairplay" indicated that every man had an equal chance at staking his claim.

BERGH HOTEL: This hotel was built before 1904.
*FAIRPLAY HOTEL: 500 Main Street, Fairplay, CO 80440; 719-836-4699; stayfairplay.com/history.

The land on which the hotel sits was bought in 1873 for $87.50 by Louis and Marie Valiton, who built the original Valiton Hotel. The hotel's name changed as the business changed hands; it burned down in 1920, forcing its closure. But by August 1921, prominent Park County citizens had rebuilt the hotel on its original foundation, following the original floor plans as closely as possible.

Architect William Bowman of Denver employed the Rustic/Adirondack–style for the hotel—fitting for its rugged mountain surroundings. By early June 1922, the new hotel had opened.

The hotel closed in 2008 but was purchased and renovated in 2010, reopening that same year. The hotel's Middle Fork Restaurant, a full-service restaurant, serves breakfast, lunch and dinner in season.

The hotel boasts eighteen rooms and a reportedly long-standing ghost named Julia. It is on the National Register of Historic Places, called the Fairplay Valiton Hotel, to acknowledge its original name, the Valiton Hotel.
*HAND HOTEL: 531 Front Street, Fairplay, CO 80440; 719-836-3595. Built in 1931 by Jake and Jesse Hand, this hotel still operates as a bed-and-breakfast, overlooking the Middle Fork of the Platte River. It is acknowledged as a haunted hotel.

Hartsel

This town was founded in 1880 and named for Samuel Hartsel, local cattle rancher. Due to its location in the center of the state, it is cleverly called the "Heart of Colorado."

HOT SPRINGS HOTEL: Built before 1907 near an area hot springs, this hotel could be reached via the Colorado Midland Railway.

The Hot Springs Hotel at Hartsel, circa 1907.

Insmont

In 1898, Harry Insley, Denver cycling enthusiast and member of the Colorado legislature, purchased land between Bailey and Estabrook to promote cycling and the great outdoors. The new retreat was named Cycle Park. Insley, president of the Denver Wheel Club, began developing his resort about the same time as other resorts like Glen Isle, Kiowa Lodge and Shawnee Lodge were being built. By 1900, Insley had moved to Cycle Park to oversee his resort. Cycle Park was soon after renamed as the town of "Insmont."

The Denver, South Park and Pacific Railroad brought guests to the area. Insley built a clubhouse called the Insmont Hotel, adding cottages for members and guests. A general store, railroad stop, icehouse and wooden racetrack for bicycle races and socials were installed. In 1902, an Insmont post office was approved. Insmont was soon accommodating the elite Denver Wheel Club, vacationers and permanent residents, and it flourished until 1909, when business fell off. In 1910, Insley sold his whole resort for $7,000, including all structures, to an East Coast investor named Martha Pauly, who divided and sold off Insmont's lots and buildings.

INSMONT HOTEL: Built in 1900, this hotel was operated by H.E. Insley in 1904.

PITKIN COUNTY

This county, named for Governor Frederick Pitkin, was called the "Shining Mountains" by the Utes. Its 975 square miles in the White River National Forest are surrounded by peaks of the Elk Range in the northern Rockies.

Ashcroft: Ghost Town

Renamed from Chloride in 1882, Ashcroft was an active mining town south of Aspen. Within in a couple of years, Ashcroft had some thirty-five hundred residents, six hotels and twenty saloons. But in 1884, a rich strike in nearby Aspen ended Ashcroft's prosperity, and people left, dragging their homes

The remains of an unnamed Ashcroft hotel.

with them. By 1890, Ashcroft had lost most of its businesses, and when the town's last resident died in 1939, it became an official ghost town. The Tenth Mountain Division used the town for training during World War II.

Aspen

An Indian uprising was technically responsible for the founding of this town. Nestled in the Rockies at 8,161 feet, Aspen was first called Ute City by miners who inadvertently established it in 1879 by remaining on the western side of the Continental divide to avoid a scalping by Utes. The settlement was renamed Aspen in 1880 and soon surpassed Leadville as the most productive silver district. But as with all mining towns, production and population declined markedly with the repeal of the Silver Act. Yet Aspen had other, untapped resources.

Entrepreneurs first explored the possibility of turning the town into a ski resort in the 1930s, but their plans were foiled by World War II. After the war, the Aspen Skiing Corporation was founded in 1946, and the town quickly became the well-known resort it is today, proving that snow was an even more valuable commodity than silver.

Hotel Jerome, Aspen. *Photo courtesy of Hotel Jerome, a RockResort.*

BURT HOUSE: This hotel was built before 1904.

CLARENDON HOTEL: This hotel was built sometime between 1880 and 1890 on a corner, with a wraparound balcony and a flat roof.

EUREKA HOUSE: This hotel was built before 1904.

*HOTEL JEROME: 330 East Main Street, Aspen, CO 81611; 970-920-1000; hoteljerome.rockresorts.com.

Hotel Jerome was built in 1889 by Jerome B. Wheeler, co-owner of New York's Macy's Department Store. It was planned in the style of the great European hotels to bring civility to what was then a raucous mining town. The hotel was one of the first buildings west of the Mississippi to be fully lit by electricity, featuring ninety rooms, fifteen baths, indoor plumbing, steam heat and a rope-pulled elevator. Following the 1890s Silver Crash, the hotel struggled to remain open. But when Aspen became a ski resort in the 1940s, the Hotel Jerome was restored and soon became a mecca for celebrities.

The hotel offers three restaurants: the Garden Terrace, the popular J-Bar and the relaxed Library, featuring locally inspired menus, sustainable cuisine and fresh, organic, natural and seasonal ingredients. With continuing updates, this elegant hotel is operating in its 122nd year.

WINDSOR HOTEL: This hotel was built about 1887.

Nast

Nast was as a resort town on the Fryingpan River, west of Hagerman Pass, accessed by the Colorado Midland Railway.

NAST HOTEL: Built sometime between 1900 and 1910, this hotel was decorated in the rustic Craftsman style. The hotel likely closed around the time of the closing of the Busk-Ivanhoe Tunnel in 1921.

The office of the Hotel Nast, circa 1910. Half-log pieces fit together to form a multitude of squares covering walls, the stairway, the front desk and benches.

Redstone

Redstone is an unincorporated community, established by John Cleveland Osgood. It is located near the ski resort town of Snowmass and is known as the "Ruby of the Rockies."

*REDSTONE INN: 82 Redstone Boulevard, Snowmass Village, CO 81623; 970-963-2526; redstoneinn.thegilmorecollection.com.

John Osgood, wealthy industrialist, did more than run a profitable mining enterprise. To improve living standards of the miners, and as a social experiment, he built eighty-four chalet-style homes in Redstone to house them. He then constructed a twenty-room lodge intended for use by bachelor employees and as a meeting place for the Colorado Fuel and Iron Company Board of Directors.

Today, the Redstone has become a magical resort in the Rockies. It, and the small mountain village located beneath the great red cliffs, is on the National Register of Historic Places.

Osgood's nearby forty-two-room estate, Cleveholm Manor, built between 1897 and 1901 (also known as Redstone Castle), is open for tours (info@redstonecastle.us).

The Redstone Inn today. *Photo courtesy of the Redstone Inn.*

RIO GRANDE COUNTY

Formed in 1874 from Conejos and Costilla Counties, this county is the gateway to the San Juan Mountains, named for the Rio Grande, which flows through it. Late in February, sand hill cranes, the San Luis Valley's oldest visitors, begin their annual trek north, stopping near the Monte Vista National Wildlife Refuge every year.

Del Norte

Founded in 1871, Del Norte is the seat of Rio Grande County, located in southern Colorado.

HOTEL EL RIO: This hotel was built before 1930.
FORK HOUSE: Built before 1904, this hotel was operated by A. Pfeifer in 1904.
LOVE HOUSE: Built before 1904, this hotel was operated by Mrs. W.H. Freeman in 1904.
WINDSOR HOTEL: 625 Grand Avenue, Del Norte, CO 81132.

Operated by D.H. Hill in 1904, this hotel, constructed shortly after the town's founding in 1871, occupies one half of a city block downtown. The Windsor was the main social and commercial center for over one hundred years. In 1993, it was saved from demolition by a local benefactor and has been partially restored.

Monte Vista

Monte Vista in the Spanish language means "Mountain View." This historic town is located in the heart of the San Luis Valley, surrounded by the Rockies.

The Monte Vista National Wildlife Refuge is one of the area's top attractions. Established by the Migratory Bird Conservation Commission in 1953, the wetland habitat provides refuge for wildlife, especially migratory birds. Ancient Native American petroglyphs in the area depict the sand hill crane's migration, confirming that these birds have used the San Luis Valley as a stopover for over two thousand years. The annual Crane Festival is held here in late February each year.

Monte Vista is near the Los Caminos Antiguos (the Ancient Roads) Scenic and Historic Byway. The route traces the Rio Grande River and meanders through the fertile San Luis Valley and some of Colorado's oldest communities, also passing the Great Sand Dunes National Monument.

Near completion in 1883, the Hotel Blanca in Monte Vista was a three-story stone building with a gambrel roof, dormers, an arcade, chimneys and arched windows.

BLANCA HOTEL: Built in 1883, this hotel burned down in 1902. Magnificent by any standards, the Blanca exuded an aura of permanence, enhancing the town and welcoming guests to its sturdy, elegant arms. But the unexpected can change everything in an instant. As with the death of a beautiful young woman, the unfortunate end of the Blanca is remembered as a tragic loss of something that should have endured for generations. Sadly, the Blanca was reduced to ruins in a blaze that occurred in November 1902.

COMMERCIAL HOTEL: Built before 1904, this hotel was operated by J.F. Anderson in 1904.

EL MONTE HOTEL: 925 First Avenue, Monte Vista, CO 81144. Built in 1930, this hotel was later renamed the Monte Villa. The rural community constructed the $112,000 hotel, designed by E. Floyd Redding. It offered all modern conveniences, including Monte Vista's first elevator.

HUNTER HOTEL: Built before 1904, this hotel was operated by Mrs. M.P. Hunter in 1904.

SIMPSON HOTEL: Built before 1904, this hotel was operated by John Hecker in 1904.

ROUTT COUNTY

Routt County was created from western Grand County in 1877 and named for John Long Routt, the last territorial and first state governor of Colorado.

Hayden

This town was named for Ferdinand Hayden, a surveyor who explored western Colorado in the late 1800s. With a history of coal mining and farming, Hayden is a quiet community near the Medicine Bow–Routt National Forest, Mount Zirkel and the Sarvis Creek Wilderness Areas, a favorite region for hiking, backpacking and other outdoor activities.

OXFORD HOTEL: Built before 1904, this hotel was operated by C.T. Bowman in 1904.

Steamboat Springs

This city, founded by James Crawford, is named for the Steamboat Spring, located near the town's library. The spring itself was named for its bubbling, which sounded like a steamboat engine to early settlers. But blasting for railroad construction in 1908 silenced the chugging spring. In the 1890s, Crawford staked a claim near the Steamboat Spring and built a cabin near Iron Spring, the community's favorite spring, due to its sweeter water. According to the book *The Cabin at Medicine Springs*, written by Crawford's daughter, Lulita Crawford Pritchett, locals made a drink from the Iron Spring's water, using lemon and syrup, calling the finished product "Steamboat Fuzz."

The Yampa River flows through the middle of town, and today two hot springs are open to the public. The largest, Old Town Hot Springs, has multiple pools and two slides. A few miles out of town is Strawberry Park Hot Springs, with two pools and natural rock formations. Strawberry Park offers stargazing opportunities due to its lack of ambient light and permits nude bathing. In recent years, Steamboat Springs has become an internationally known winter resort and skiing destination.

BARTZ HOTEL: Built before 1904, this hotel was operated by Mrs. Alice Bartz in 1904.
LA VETA HOTEL: This hotel was built before 1904.
ONYX HOTEL: This hotel was built before 1904 and operated by Gardner & Co. in 1904.

SHERIDAN HOTEL: Built before 1904, this hotel was operated by Mrs. L. McGettegan in 1904.

STEAMBOAT CABIN HOTEL: Built in 1909, this hotel burned down in 1939. This hotel was built across from the Iron Spring and had one hundred rooms but only four bathrooms. Despite promoting the area springs as a health spa, the hotel was never fully successful. It changed hands several times, closing for periods of time, before reopening in 1937 for a convention. In 1939, fire destroyed the Steamboat Cabin Hotel, taking the lives of two people. The town library now occupies the site.

Yampa

This town, incorporated in 1906, was named for the local native Yampa plant. Yampa is reportedly a Ute word meaning "bear." In the early 1900s, the railroad transported Yampa's cattle, produce and lumber to market, and today the town's economy is based on agriculture. Yampa has preserved many of its historic buildings.

The Antlers Hotel, Yampa, circa 1899.

Hotel Yampa. This hotel was a U-shaped log house with a sod roof and an elk horn fence in front. It was the residence of Ira Van Camp, who ran the stage station and livery stable.

THE ANTLERS HOTEL: This hotel was built before 1899 on Moffatt Avenue.
MONTE CRISTO HOTEL: This hotel was built before 1902 on Moffatt Avenue, next to the Antlers Hotel.
MONTGOMERY'S HOTEL: Built before 1904, this hotel was operated by Mrs. Montgomery in 1904.
ROYAL HOTEL: This hotel was built before 1909.
HOTEL YAMPA: This hotel was built between 1880 and 1900.

SAGUACHE COUNTY

"Saquache," pronounced "Sa-watch," comes from a Ute word meaning "Water at Blue Earth." At an elevation of seventy-eight hundred feet, Saguache is the northern gateway to the San Luis Valley, surrounded by the Sangre de Cristos on the east and the San Juan range on the west, with many fourteen-thousand-foot peaks.

The area was settled in 1867 by Otto Mears, who operated the first toll road above Poncha Pass. Today, cattle and sheep are raised there, and there is some logging on Forest Service land. Farming is done in the lower valley, where crops include potatoes, lettuce and barley.

Crestone

Crestone is a small settlement at the foot of the western slope of the Sangre de Cristos. Named for the fourteen-thousand-foot peaks east of town, Crestone began as a small mining town.

More recently, the Crestone area has become a spiritual center, representing various religions, including a Carmelite monastery, a Hindu temple, a Zen Buddhist center, several Tibetan centers and a variety of New Age activities.

HOTEL CRESTONE: Built before 1904, this hotel was operated by Jones & Sloan in 1904.

Villa Grove

This town was settled in 1865 by Colorado Civil War veterans. In 1880, news of the silver strike just over the hill in Bonanza brought Ulysses S. Grant around to look into silver prospects. But the ore was low grade, and by 1900, most of the miners had moved on.

Villa Grove's original site was the southern terminus of the Denver and Rio Grande narrow gauge railroad over Poncha Pass. The town was originally named Garibaldi, after Italian revolutionary Giuseppe Garibaldi, and in 1870, Garibaldi was granted a post office. But in 1872, its name was changed to the less political Villa Grove. After train service was curtailed in 1890, the town declined and is today a quiet community in the northern San Luis Valley.

VALLEY VIEW HOT SPRINGS: This hotel was operated by J. Stewart in 1904. The springs, noted for curative properties, were located one mile from the Denver and Rio Grande Station.

SUMMIT COUNTY

Summit County was formed in 1861. As with most counties in this part of the state, its early history was written by the gold rush and the mining industry.

Breckenridge

Breckenridge was founded in 1859 to serve miners working gold deposits along the Blue River. General George Spencer chose the name "Breckinridge" for John C. Breckinridge, vice president of the United States. But in 1861, when the former vice president joined the Confederates as a brigadier general, the town's Union-sympathizing residents altered its name to Breckenridge, changing the first "i" to an "e."

Breckenridge is the location of the former home of civil rights pioneer Barney Ford, whose house is now the Barney Ford House Museum at 111 East Washington Avenue.

Since 1981, the town has hosted the Breckenridge Festival of Film.

ARLINGTON HOUSE: This hotel was built between 1880 and 1900 on Main Street.
COLORADO HOTEL: This hotel was built before 1904.
DENVER HOTEL: This hotel was built about 1889.
SILVERTHORN HOTEL: This hotel was built before 1860.

Dillon

In the late 1800s, the first town of Dillon was located in the deepest part of Lake Dillon. It was then a trading post with a few cabins at the juncture of three rivers. But as Denver grew, needing water from the high country, Dillon was forced to relocate for the reservoir that would

The Hamilton Hotel in snow, circa 1898.

become known as Lake Dillon. Dillon moved to the present northeast shore of Lake Dillon, with the reservoir's completion in 1963. Some of its buildings were moved to Silverthorne, including the general store and post office. In the 1960s, when skiing became an economic factor, businesses again located in Dillon, and today the town is a short distance from many world-class ski areas.

HAMILTON HOTEL: Built before 1898, this hotel was operated by J.D. McGrew in 1904.

ORO GRANDE HOTEL: Built before 1904, this hotel was operated by Mrs. G. Williams in 1904.

WARREN HOUSE: Built before 1904, this hotel was operated by C.C. Warren in 1904.

Frisco

This town was founded in 1873 by Henry Recen, developing fast due to the area's many mines. Enter Henry Learned, railroad agent representing the State of Colorado, who was hired by rail companies interested in expanding rail lines west. One such stakeholder was the St. Louis–San Francisco Railway, also called the Frisco Line. In 1875, Learned nailed a sign on a cabin in town and declared the area "Frisco City" in hopes of drawing the railroad line to the area.

Frisco was not named for San Francisco, California. Its name came from Learned's combination of letters taken from the St. Louis–San Francisco Railway Company's logo: the "Fr" from Francisco, the "is" from St. Louis and the "co" from Company.

But Learned's clever plan failed, and ironically, the Frisco Line wound up running south from Missouri to Frisco, Texas. Nevertheless, Learned remained in the area and became a community leader. By 1882, Frisco (which had dropped "City") was served by both the Denver, South Park and Pacific Railroad and the Denver and Rio Grande Railroad.

Frisco's mining boom lasted until 1918, and although the mines still produced some, the town was hard hit by the Depression. By 1930, Frisco's population had dwindled to eighteen, and many smaller, less accessible mining towns were abandoned. But Frisco's perseverance paid off; its population rose to fifty in 1946. With twenty-five hundred current residents, Frisco is skating into a prosperous future thanks to the ski industry, which attracts some three million people a year to the area.

The Frisco Lodge, the first building on right, circa 1890s. *Photo courtesy of the Frisco Lodge.*

*FRISCO LODGE: 321 Main Street, PO Box 1325, Frisco, CO 80443; 970-668-0195, 800-279-6000.

Originally a stagecoach stop, this lodge soon became a way station for passengers and crew on the Denver and Rio Grande Railroad. The Frisco Lodge continues to occupy the same building, its rooms decorated to retain the ambiance of the period. The Frisco Lodge, now a bed-and-breakfast, has been in continuous operation since the 1880s.

Montezuma

This town began as a mining camp, at an elevation of 10,200 feet, named for Montezuma, emperor of the Aztecs. It was founded by miners in 1865 after silver was discovered in nearby Argentine Pass. Incorporating in 1881, at one time it supported two hotels but declined following the 1893 silver bust. Located near the west side of Loveland Pass, it is often considered a ghost town but has kept a small population over the years. Five major fires have decimated much of the town, including two that razed many of its historic structures, among them the Summit House.

ROCKY MOUNTAIN HOUSE: This hotel was built before 1910.
SUMMIT HOUSE: This hotel was built before 1900 and burned down in 1958.

WESTERN COUNTIES

The significance of railroads in developing the West may be overlooked today, with super highways and airlines now the primary movers. But over a century ago, railroads held significant power over the land their rails traversed. More than a few towns were founded by railroads, some having been planned or actually moved to specific locations, autocratically predetermined by railroad officials. Land speculation, as practiced by railroads, was quite lucrative, seldom failing to establish a healthy base for rail expansion. Conversely, towns dried up if the railroads departed.

The other driving force in settling the West, when mining was not involved, was agriculture. Farming and ranching continue to be significant factors in western Colorado and still support numerous thriving communities.

DELTA COUNTY

Delta County was created in 1883 from portions of central Gunnison County. In an unusual twist, the county was named for the town of Delta.

Delta

Delta is located where the Uncompahgre and Gunnison Rivers meet, just west of Black Canyon of the Gunnison, where the river has carved twenty-nine-hundred-foot gorges. It began as a trading post for Utes and whites,

The Delta House transfer wagon, Main St., Delta, CO. 1896.

and every September, the Council Tree Pow Wow American Indian Cultural Festival is held at Confluence Park. The town is known for the murals on the walls of its buildings and the paintings on its canyon walls and has been called the "City of Murals."

Fossil enthusiasts should not miss Dry Mesa Quarry, site of the first discovery of Brachiosaurus and Ultrasaurus bones. Set in the Uncompahgre National Forest, the quarry is one of the most famous dinosaur locales in the world. Seventeen different species have been discovered there since 1971 (call 970-874-6638 for information).

DELTA HOUSE: Built before 1904, this hotel was operated by William Shaver in 1904.

SHEARMAN HOUSE: No information available.

Hotchkiss

The North Fork of the Gunnison River Valley was isolated until 1880, when the Ute Indian reservation was closed following the Meeker Massacre. Utes were forced to move to two small reservations in northern Utah and southwest Colorado, making way for white settlers in the North Fork area. The first to come was a small group from the Lake City area, led by Enos Hotchkiss, who discovered the Golden Fleece mine. His group secretly scouted the valley, choosing prime land illegally, prior to the Utes' removal. In 1881, Hotchkiss returned with the two Duke brothers, four other adventurers—Clark, Angevine, Wade and Platt— and several hundred horses. These were the first legal settlers in the valley; Hotchkiss and the Dukes staked homesteads near present-day Hotchkiss.

Three of Hotchkiss's other companions settled farther away, while Platt reportedly went insane and was either sent home or shot. Precision in news was sketchy in those days. But the area's main source of revenue would eventually become coal mining. Since the railroad came to North Fork in 1902, coal has been significant to Hotchkiss's economy. Local coal is hard anthracite, cleaner burning than bituminous coal and much in demand for the nation's power plants.

DOWDY SPRINGS HOTEL: Built before 1904, this hotel was operated by M. Dowdy in 1904.

HOTCHKISS HOTEL: Built before 1894, this hotel was operated by Evan Morton in 1904.

Paonia

This area was first explored in 1853 by Captain John Gunnison on an expedition to locate a pass through the Rockies. After the Ute Reservation was closed in 1880, the area was settled by Samuel Wade and William Clark, Enos Hotchkiss's companions. Paonia was incorporated in 1902. Wade had brought peony roots with him to Colorado, inspiring him to suggest the peony's Latin name, *Paeonia*, for the town's name. The post office would not allow the extra vowel, so "Paeonia" became "Paonia."

*THE BROSS HOTEL: 312 Onarga Street, Paonia, CO 81428; 970-527-6776; www.paonia-inn.com.

This hotel was built and run by William Bross and his wife, Laura, in 1906. The Bross was reported to be "the only really first-class hotel in the county." This was largely due to its fireproof, triple-brick construction and the upscale amenities for its day. Located one block from the town's main street, the hotel operated for many years under a succession of owners.

Ghost-hunting guests might experience a visit from "Mother Bross," seen sitting on beds and moving objects. Several years ago, after an innkeeper had made a derogatory comment about Mrs. Bross, a large mirror fell to the floor without breaking. An apology to Mrs. Bross allowed the mirror to remain hanging on the wall.

The Bross Hotel. *Drawing by Pam Archer. Courtesy of the Bross Hotel.*

In the mid-1990s, the inn was renovated, and today it maintains the charm of an old hotel, plus modern amenities and comforts. Now a bed-and-breakfast, the Bross Hotel offers ten guest rooms, holds special Mystery Nights and afternoon teas and is once again Delta County's premier hotel.

PAONIA HOTEL: Built before 1904, this hotel was operated by C.J. Classon in 1904.

DOLORES COUNTY

Dolores County was created in 1881 from western portions of Ouray County and was named for the Dolores River. While Dolores is an economically poor county, it has a wealth of human history. It has been inhabited since at least 2500 BC, its western portions densely populated from AD 900 to 1300. Some ten thousand people are thought to have lived in area villages. But by the 1500s, this population was either destroyed or had moved away following severe drought and disturbances in its society. For centuries afterward, the county was home to nomadic tribes, including Utes and Navajos. As in much of southwest Colorado, Dolores County has many Anasazi ruins and, according to the Anasazi Heritage Center, more than eight hundred recorded sites.

The county also contains a portion of the historic Dominguez-Escalante Trail of 1776, marking the eighteen-hundred-mile trip intended to discover an overland route between Santa Fe, New Mexico, and Monterey, California. The expedition camped on Dove Creek in the western portion of the county.

White trappers were in the eastern mountains by 1832–33, and gold was discovered in 1866. But it was not until the Utes were removed by the Brunot Agreement in 1878 that legalized mining began. Nevertheless, the Pioneer Mining District was illegally established in 1876 in the Rico area, with large silver deposits found there in 1879.

By 1890, the Rio Grande Southern Railway connected Dolores County to Durango, Telluride and Ridgway, until the tracks were eventually abandoned in 1952. In the 1870s, cattle ranching began in the western part of the county, which never had rail service. Before long, overgrazing of grasses caused proliferation of sagebrush, piñon and juniper. But by 1914, as dry land farming expanded, homesteading began, and today crops of pinto beans and winter wheat are still a foundation of the local economy.

With the development of irrigation and the construction of the McPhee Reservoir, county agriculture has been given more options. Nevertheless, in 2009, Dolores achieved notoriety as the most economically depressed county in Colorado.

Rico

When Rico was originally chosen as the county seat, its first courthouse was a modest log cabin, replaced by a stone and brick courthouse in 1883. But the county seat moved to Dove Creek in 1946, and the original county courthouse in Rico became the town hall.

In 1892, its mining district held more than five thousand people, three times the current population of the county. But the silver panic hit the town hard, and by 1900, the population had shrunk to fewer than one hundred. Dolores County has seen its booms and busts. Rico counted only forty-five residents in 1974. But with the advent of skiing, the town has rebounded.

HOTEL RHODE: Built before 1904, this hotel was operated by C.W. Rhode in 1904.

GARFIELD COUNTY

This county was named for President James Garfield and is known for its marble and coal mining, agriculture and tourism.

Carbondale

Located on the Roaring Fork River between Aspen and Glenwood Springs, this town takes its name from Cardondale, Pennsylvania, home of some of the town's early founders. Once a potato-growing community to supply food to miners, it has become a bedroom community for nearby Aspen.

HOTEL CARBONDALE: Built before 1900, this hotel was operated by F.W. Lindauer in 1904 on a prominent street corner. The solid brick structure housed retail businesses, with signs advertising them and "Hotel, Strictly Modern."

Glenwood Springs

The town of Defiance was first settled in 1881 by Isaac Cooper, whose dream of turning it into a resort did not materialize in his lifetime. The town marks the confluence of Roaring Fork and the Colorado River, 180 miles west of Denver, and is now famous for its hot sulfur springs.

In hopes of making her environment more familiar, Cooper's wife, Sarah, struggling to adjust to frontier life, persuaded the town to change its name to Glenwood Springs for her hometown of Glenwood, Iowa. But in 1883, the town was still Defiance, a rough tent settlement near today's Seventh Street. Although its crude structures were replaced by more acceptable ones in the early 1900s, most businesses on the block remained saloons and brothels catering to miners, and it would take Prohibition to clean up the neighborhood.

In 1904, a red sandstone and brick depot replaced the original train station on the river. The new depot was built to match the sixteenth-century Italian architecture of the Glenwood Hot Springs and Hotel Colorado. But the station's location remained near the riverfront's rough neighborhood, and President Taft refused to enter Glenwood from the depot due to its proximity to the infamous bar and red-light district.

Glenwood Springs' unique location at the juncture of two rivers, and its stop on the railroad, made it a growing center of commerce. It became the first town of its size in the United States to be fully wired for electricity.

The first Colorado Hotel, 1885.

The town has seen numerous famous visitors, including Presidents Taft, Hoover and Teddy Roosevelt, who spent an entire vacation living out of the historic Hotel Colorado. Doc Holliday, Wild West legend from the OK Corral, passed the final months of his life in town and is buried in its early cemetery.

COLORADO HOTEL: This hotel was built before 1885.
*HOTEL COLORADO: 526 Pine Street, Glenwood Springs, CO 81601; 970-945-6511, 888-599-2752; hotelcolorado.com.

In 1872, Princeton engineering graduate Walter B. Devereux arrived in the mining camp of Aspen, where he and his two brothers became wealthy from silver, coal and other minerals. Devereux had been told by Kit Carson of the curative waters of Yampah Springs, used for centuries by the Ute Indians. Once Devereux came to the valley now known as Glenwood Springs, he liked what he saw and bought ten acres, including the springs. Its development would await the arrival of the railroad.

Construction on Hotel Colorado began in 1891 and was completed in 1893. Designed by Edward Lippincott Tilton from the New York firm of Boring, Tilton and Mellon, the magnificent hotel was inspired by the Villa de Medici. Sandstone from Colorado's Frying Pan River, combined with Roman brick, gave the dramatic building its stately, singular appearance.

Located on the hill above the European-styled Hot Springs Spa, the magnificent new resort drew the wealthy as well as the ailing and became a playground for the new American aristocracy. The hotel featured a U-shaped plan with twin bell towers and a first-floor arched gallery. Opening in 1893, Hotel Colorado brought celebrities from all over the world, appealing to a diverse clientele. Devereux, the silver baron, did not stint on his "Grande Dame." The south court, which is now a courtyard, once held a large pool with an electrically lit imported fountain, shooting a 185-foot jet of water, higher than the two bell towers. At one time, from the existing lounge, a 12-foot-wide sheet of water dropped 25 feet into a pool beneath it. Strategically placed lights and colored glass gave the appearance of falling rainbows. In mornings, guests could sit by the pool and catch trout for breakfast.

In 1905, Hotel Colorado welcomed President Theodore Roosevelt and his party for a three-week bear hunting expedition. Previously, in 1901, the then vice president had hunted mountain lion on Keystone Ranch near Meeker. It was reported that Roosevelt hung over a cliff to shoot a wounded lion between the eyes. Roosevelt was so impressed by the Glenwood Springs resort that he returned to Hotel Colorado many times, giving an address from its balcony and making the hotel his headquarters during his presidential campaign. The Roosevelt Suite is named in honor of his stay, earning the hotel the title of the "Little White House."

According to legend, the venerable teddy bear was "born" at Hotel Colorado. To cheer Roosevelt after an unsuccessful hunt, hotel maids gave him a stuffed bear pieced from cloth scraps. Roosevelt's daughter Alyce is reported to have said, "I will call it Teddy." Another version says that a reporter, upon hearing of the stuffed bear, coined it the "Teddy Bear." Either way, enter that universally appealing toy. An enterprising toy maker wrote to Roosevelt, asking for and receiving permission to use "Teddy" for marketing the bears, and Ideal Novelty and Toy began distributing them in 1903.

Glenwood had one of the first motion pictures made of a president, but it was too shocking for release because some "painted ladies of the night" managed to sneak in and be photographed meeting Roosevelt. Upon developing the film, it was discovered that one "lady" was wearing an indecent riding habit, and the film was destroyed.

In 1909, President Taft arrived, a parade of carriages bringing him and his entourage to the hotel. When offered private use of the Hot Springs pool, Taft declined, stating that it was better that a man of his size not bathe in public.

Fortunes blossomed in the West in those days. One whose wealth was the result of her husband's gold strike was Molly Brown (who had become "Unsinkable"). She visited the Hotel Colorado to relax following her odyssey on the *Titanic*. One of the hotel's Tower Suites, the Molly Brown Suite is decorated as a tribute to this dynamic woman and is appointed with her family photos, memorabilia and period furnishings.

The hotel has a long history of unexplained psychic phenomena and is a favorite spot for spook hunters. Both towers and other areas of the hotel are reportedly haunted. One invisible tenant of the Colorado likes to do interior decorating. During a 1982 renovation, new wallpaper was being installed in Room 551. The next day, the newly applied paper had been taken down and rolled neatly on the floor. The wallpaper was again placed on the walls, only to be found on the floor the next day. Eventually, several paper samples were placed on the bed. The next morning, all but one sample had been put on the floor. When that "chosen" paper was pasted on the walls, it remained in place.

During the Roaring Twenties, a cast of dubious characters, including Al Capone and Legs Diamond, found the Hotel Colorado to their liking. A special front-door awning was installed so their ilk could enter the hotel unnoticed. In 1939, President Hoover visited the hotel. In 1942, under the auspices of the U.S. Navy, the hotel was used as a hospital for injured soldiers

The Hotel Colorado today. *Photo courtesy of the Hotel Colorado.*

during World War II. The hotel features the Courtyard Café, the Cedar Banks Room and Baron's Restaurant. Delicious dishes are prepared from locally grown produce and meats; fresh Colorado trout is a favorite. Menus offer seasonal cocktails and desserts, including the iconic American red velvet cake, prepared by the hotel's British pastry chef. The hotel has been on the National Register of Historic Places since 1977.

For a historic journey back to the time of Teddy Roosevelt and a rare chance to experience the authentic grace and glamour of Colorado's gilded age, the Hotel Colorado is the history seeker's perfect destination.

*HOTEL DENVER: 402 Seventh Street, Glenwood Springs, CO 81601; 970-945-6565, 800-826-8820; thehoteldenver.com.

In 1906, young Italian immigrant Henry Bosco established a bottling company in the basement of the raunchy saloons facing the depot, where the brewery is located now. This was a strategic move, for in addition to nine saloons on his block, there were at least fourteen others within a one-block radius. Henry acquired the saloon above his business, later purchased another adjacent bar and, in 1914, built the Star Hotel. Meanwhile, at the block's west end, the enterprising Art Kendrick opened a second-rate rooming house called the Denver Rooms to appeal to Denver clientele.

Prohibition in 1921 devastated the saloon and red-light district. But fortunately for Bosco and Kendrick, local real estate became so depressed that both men were able to add to their holdings and expand their hotels, to the point that they eventually adjoined each other. Bosco's nephew, Mike, acquired the Star Hotel after World War I, and in 1938, he acquired Kendrick's Denver Rooms. The two properties combined into what is now the Hotel Denver.

The hotel is in possession of a rare historic piece of art. According to Rock Island Railroad officials, fifty mother-of-pearl pictures were created shortly after the turn of the century and given to hotels such as the Hotel Denver as a promotion. Rock Island paid fifty dollars each for these pictures, made by the Western Sand Blast Company in Chicago. Each was handcrafted individually with mother-of-pearl inlay; no two were alike. Their backgrounds are also unique, as they were painted free hand. Other known locations for these pictures are the BROADMOOR Hotel in Colorado Springs and the Smithsonian Institute.

HOTEL GLENWOOD: Built before 1885, this hotel was located at Eighth and Grand and was operated by W.R. Lee in 1904.

GRAND HOTEL: Built before 1904, this hotel was operated by J.R. Phillipi in 1904.

PALACE HOTEL: Built before 1904, this hotel was operated by S.W. Smart in 1904.

STAR HOTEL: This hotel was built in 1914 by Henry Bosco.

New Castle

This town was founded by Jasper Ward, a freight supplier, whose dirt-floor cabin on Elk Creek became the town post office. Ward, a friend of Ute chief Colorow, became deputy sheriff, riding with a posse to calm a Ute uprising following the Meeker Massacre. He was killed at age thirty-seven during a conflict between Utes and the Colorado National Guard in 1887.

The town was first known as Grand Buttes and then Chapman, but it was incorporated as New Castle in 1888. It was named by English miners for Newcastle-on-Tyne, an English town known for its coal mines.

New Castle calls itself the "Gateway to the Western Colorado Rockies." Located twelve miles west of Glenwood Springs, its population was eighteen hundred in the 1890s. Its active coal industry served Aspen and Leadville smelters via the Colorado Midland and the Denver and Rio Grande Railroads. Local mines produced high-quality coal but also methane gas. In 1896, the Vulcan Mine suffered a violent explosion, sending timbers into the Colorado River and killing almost fifty miners. A second devastating explosion in 1913 killed thirty-seven, ending most mining efforts in the area. Residents turned to agriculture for a living.

New Castle is the site of an underground mine fire, smoldering since 1899, known as Burning Mountain. Such fires can burn for hundreds of years, venting through natural cracks in the earth. In 2002, the 1899 fire sparked what became known as the Coal Seam Fire, burning 12,209 acres. The fire destroyed twenty-nine homes, a commercial structure and fourteen outbuildings, forcing evacuation of West Glenwood Springs and parts of New Castle. Steam coming from the vent is still visible today.

In July, New Castle hosts its annual Burning Mountain Days Festival.

ALBANY HOTEL: Built before 1904, this hotel was operated by C.A. Hahn in 1904.
NOREN HOTEL: Built before 1904, this hotel was operated by C.H. Noren & Son in 1904.

LA PLATA COUNTY

Named for the La Plata River and La Plata Mountains, this county is the site of the Durango Rock Shelters of the Anasazi culture. "La plata" is the Spanish word for silver.

Durango

Gold was discovered in 1860 in the San Juan Mountains north of present-day Durango. The Animas Valley swarmed with people hoping to strike it rich, and many built homes, making a living by supplying the mining camps. The Civil War slowed southwestern Colorado's expansion, but the arrival of the railroads changed area history. In 1880, railroad officials drew plans for the town of Durango, laying out the rails, depot and rail yards, as well many of its first streets. Drawn by the abundance of silver and gold ore, the Denver and Rio Grande Railroad came to serve the San Juan mining district in 1881, organizing Durango as a town the same year. The city is named for Durango, Mexico, which in turn was named for Durango, Spain. The word "Durango" originates from a Basque word, "Urango," which translates to "Water Town." Within a year, Durango boasted 134 businesses, many professionals and newspapers. One of its first papers, the *Durango Record*, was run by fearless crusader Caroline Romney. She referred to Durango as "the wonder of the Southwest," fiercely supporting women's right to vote.

Of primary importance to Durango's growth was completion of the forty-five-mile-long branch from Durango to Silverton, built in haste to transport all that "silver by the ton." Silverton's many mining camps were previously isolated, dependent on toll roads and pack animals to haul their ore over the Continental Divide.

Durango and its surrounding area was the location for a number of films in the 1940s and '50s, among them *Around the World in Eighty Days, Across the Wide Missouri, The Naked Spur* and *Night Passage*. At that time, Durango was known as the Hollywood of the Rockies.

The creation of Mesa-Verde National Park in 1906 to preserve ruins of the Ancestral Puebloan culture brought Durango an influx of tourists. In the 1950s, Fort Lewis College opened in Durango and is now a four-year college. In 1965, Purgatory ski resort, now known as Durango Mountain Resort, opened north of town, helping establish the area as a vacation destination. Durango is an outdoor paradise, offering skiing, hiking, kayaking, hunting, fishing, snowshoeing and bicycling. It is also known for the Durango and Silverton Narrow Gauge Railroad, running from Durango to Silverton on steam-powered trains dating from the 1920s and earlier.

COLUMBIAN HOTEL: This hotel was built in 1893 by Henry Strater next door to the Strater Hotel to intentionally compete with it. Operated by C.E. Applegate, it closed in 1895 due to the silver panic. Later, it joined the Strater.

The Grand Central Hotel nearing completion. It was built of brick of two different colors, circa 1889.

EDELMAN HOUSE: Built before 1904, this hotel was operated by H. Edelman in 1904.

*GENERAL PALMER HOTEL: 567 Main Avenue, Durango, CO 81301; 970-247-4747, 866-538-0187; generalpalmer.com.

This Victorian hotel was named for General Palmer, who also built the Durango–Silverton Narrow Gauge Railroad. Palmer is also one of the founders of Colorado Springs. The General Palmer's handsome period furnishings and historic ambiance bring the visitor back to the time of Durango's early years. The hotel is located in the heart of Durango's historic district and is listed on the National Registry of Historic Places. For the past thirty-five years, the hotel has held a AAA rating as a Four Diamond establishment.

GRAND CENTRAL HOTEL: Originally built prior to 1880 by Thomas Rockwood, this hotel was destroyed by fire in July 1889. Rebuilt of brick, it was operated by R. Kremmling in 1904. It was considered one of the town's better hotels.

HERMOSA HOUSE: Built before 1904, this hotel burned down in 1931. It was operated by C.C. Murray in 1904.

In 1874, Frank Trimble, suffering injuries from the Indian Wars, moved to land a few miles north of present-day Durango and began bathing in

T.D. Burns's Hermosa House, Trimble Hot Springs, circa 1910.

the local spring waters. Declaring that the waters had healed him, in 1882, he built a two-story hotel with fourteen guest rooms. But the first hotel burned down in 1892. T.D. Burns took over the springs and built the elegant Hermosa House in 1896, which unfortunately burned down in 1931. The springs were sold, and nine thousand bricks from the Hermosa House were used to build arched porches on a new building. In 1937, the Piccoli family purchased Trimble Hot Springs, which they ran as a popular nightclub. They also brought exotic dancers and gambling to the area, to mixed reviews.

During World War II, Trimble Hot Springs closed. The property changed hands many times until, in 1957, the third building burned down. The property has in recent years been reopened as a spa. Elders from the Southern Ute tribe were asked to bless this latest chapter of the springs' history, now called Trimble Spa and Hot Springs (6475 County Road 203, Durango, CO 81301; 970-247-0111).

INTER-OCEAN HOTEL: Built before 1904, this hotel was operated by Charles Fleck in 1904.

The NATIONAL HOTEL: This hotel was built before 1892.

PALACE HOTEL: Built about 1890–03 at 505 Main Street, this hotel was operated by W.D. McNuley in 1904. Its rooms have become part of the General Palmer Hotel. The Palace is no longer a hotel but is now a beautiful gourmet restaurant, the Palace Restaurant (970-247-2018).

*THE ROCHESTER HOTEL/PEEPLES HOTEL: 726 East Second Avenue, Durango, CO 81301; 970-385-4356, 800-664-1920; rochesterhotel.com.

The hotel opened in 1892 as the Peeples Hotel, named for one of the property's early owners. It was sold a year later to Jerry Sullivan, who in turn sold it in 1905 to Mary Frances Finn, who renamed it the Rochester. Finn added indoor baths and enlarged the building.

The hotel changed hands repeatedly, gradually falling into disrepair until its present owners, Diane and Fred Wildfang, and their son, Kirk Komick, purchased it in 1992. Under their ownership, a century after its opening, the hotel was extensively rebuilt and restored. Original hardware and woodwork were retained wherever possible, and a grand lobby was created, including an open stairway with both original and replicated banisters. Its fifteen guest rooms are named for the many movies filmed in the Durango area. The Rochester is today a beautifully renovated historic hotel; its rooms offer private baths, high ceilings, period furniture and a charming courtyard.

Since the Rochester's restoration, the Wildfangs and Komick have restored several other properties on the street and have helped to inspire the area's revitalization.

THE SAVOY HOTEL: No information available.

*THE STRATER HOTEL: 699 Main Avenue, Durango, CO 81301; 970-247-4431, 800-247-4431; strater.com.

Cleveland pharmacist Henry Strater believed that Durango needed a grand hotel but had three strikes against him. He lacked money, had no experience and was too young to legally borrow cash. No problem. He just lied about his age and took out a loan. With the help of family and his infectious enthusiasm, Strater's dream became a reality, and $70,000 later, the Strater Hotel opened. The extraordinary edifice was constructed of 376,000 native red bricks, ornamented by hand-carved sandstone cornices and sills.

The Strater became a winter retreat for locals, who would close their homes and move into the hotel. Rooms were equipped with wood-burning stoves and comfortable furniture; some had pianos and washstands. The washstands served double duty, their cabinets containing a "facility" that would be emptied by maids. The innovative hotel also contained a strategically designed three-story privy.

The Rochester Hotel today. *Courtesy of the Rochester Hotel.*

The elegant Hotel Strater in its second century. *Photo courtesy of the Hotel Strater.*

Strater placed his pharmacy in a prominent corner of the building, and having no desire to run the hotel, leased the Strater to proprietor H.L. Rice. But Strater soon realized he had failed to exclude his pharmacy in the lease to Rice, who charged Strater exorbitant rent. Infuriated, Strater built the competing Columbian Hotel in 1893, intending to put Rice out of business. Competition between the two hotels continued until 1895, when the silver panic put them both out of business.

Following the devastation of the silver panic, the Bank of Cleveland repossessed the Strater, selling it to Ms. Hattie Mashburn and Charles E. Stillwell, who operated the hotel until 1926, refining its appeal by offering opera and fine dining. During the Roaring Twenties, James A. Jarvis introduced the movie industry.

In 1926, a group of Durango businessmen, led by banker Earl A. Barker Sr., bought the hotel, refreshing its image. Townspeople no longer retreated to the Strater in winter, but many notables made the Strater their home away from home. Western author Louis L'Amour always asked for Room 222, above the Diamond Belle Saloon, claiming that its honky-tonk music helped set the mood for his writing. Today, Room 222 is known as the Louis L'Amour Room.

The Strater continues to upgrade with the times. Under Jentra and Earl Barker Jr., the hotel underwent "invisible" renovations, attending to details such as baths, air conditioning, heat, modern amenities and telephone service. Current president Roderick E. Barker has overseen installation of fine woodwork and authentic Bradbury and Bradbury wallpapers, reflecting the Victorian period. Windowed showcases brimming with antique collectibles are located throughout.

With elegance as a byword, the charms of the Strater have only increased with age, as in its 113th year, this grand hotel continues to welcome guests with the grace and hospitality that have become its trademarks.

MESA COUNTY

Western Colorado was once a flood plain with a humid climate and a home to dinosaurs, whose bones are today an attraction for tourists and scientists. The first known humans in this area were the Fremont Indians, living here from AD 250 to 1300. They were hunters, farmers and artists, whose pictographs and petroglyphs remain. Mesa County, 174 miles west of Denver, was named for the area's many large mesas, including Grand

Mesa, the most extensive on earth. The county was created in 1883 from neighboring counties, with Grand Junction as its county seat.

De Beque

Located at Grand Mesa Lakes, De Beque was the historic home of the Ute Indians until whites arrived in 1880. The town was named for Dr. W.A.E. De Beque, who explored the area with a small party in 1884, seeking a location for a ranch. The town had long been a place of wild horse roundups and sales; this local history is commemorated by a mustang statue near the town hall. In 2001, De Beque became the only Wild Horse Sanctuary City in the West. The town undertakes projects in cooperation with the Bureau of Land Management and private organizations to protect the area's remaining wild horses and burros. It has constructed a public corral for the care of ailing mustangs and burros awaiting adoption. Each August, the town hosts Wild Horse Days, featuring a rodeo and parade.

HOTEL DELANO: Built before 1904, this hotel was operated by F.W. Delano in 1904.

GRAND VALLEY HOTEL: Built before 1904, this hotel was operated by Mrs. C.J. Smith in 1904.

Fruita

Fruita was established in 1884 by William Pabor, who probably never foresaw that his town would become the site of an annual May festival celebrating Mike the Headless Chicken, who lived for eighteen months after his head was cut off. Lloyd Olsen, chicken owner, would give him food and water with an eyedropper. Fortunately, this dubious event is balanced by Fruita's long-standing Fall Festival in September, which began in 1910 as a harvest event and is now a major celebration.

MCGINNIS HOTEL: Built before 1904, this hotel was operated by H.H. McGinnis in 1904.

OWENS HOTEL: Built before 1904, this hotel was operated by N. Owens in 1904.

HOTEL PARK: Built before 1904, this hotel was operated by Mrs. W.H. Pollock in 1904.

Grand Junction

Grand Junction, the Mesa County seat, is the largest city in western Colorado. Its location at the confluence of the Colorado and Gunnison Rivers has given it the nickname "River City." Until 1821, the Grand Valley was part of Spain. When western Colorado became part of Mexico in 1821, the land was opened to trappers and traders but remained the historical home of the Utes until whites arrived in the 1880s. In recent years, several local wineries have been established. The Colorado National Monument, a dramatic series of canyons and mesas, overlooks the city.

BRUNSWICK HOTEL: Built in 1886, this hotel was later torn down.
BUENA VISTA HOTEL: Built before 1904, this hotel was operated by Joseph Sanderson in 1904.
HOTEL CRANFORD: This hotel was built before 1900.
GRAND HOTEL: Built before 1887, this hotel was operated by E.W. Jordan in 1904. An 1887 trolley car advertisement snidely boasted, "The Brunswick closed! All traveling men staying at the Grand Hotel, strictly first-class."

The New Castle Stage stopped in front of the Brunswick Hotel, 1889.

Whitewater

Whitewater is a small town outside Grand Junction, near the Colorado National Monument. It is known for inspiring canyons and high desert forests.

WHITEWATER HOTEL: Built before 1904, this hotel was operated by B.T. Wright in 1904.

MOFFAT COUNTY

Moffat, created from part of Routt County in 1911 and named for David Moffat, Colorado railroad tycoon, is the farthest northwest county in Colorado. The Denver, Northwestern and Pacific Railroad attempted to build a route from Denver to Salt Lake City, but in 1913, a reorganized railroad—the Denver and Salt Lake—only reached as far Craig.

Craig

A true town of the Old West, Craig has been home to Indians, cowboys, gunfighters and mountain men. In the 1879s, Craig attracted both settlers and outlaws running from the law. Among them were Butch Cassidy, the Sundance Kid and the Wild Bunch. Craig is the site of over three hundred ancient Native American pictographs, and one of the largest herds of elk in North America still ranges in the area.

THE BAKER: Built before 1904 on Yampa Street, this hotel was operated by C.E. Baker in 1904.
THE ROYAL: Built before 1894, this hotel was operated by E.A. Collett.

MONTEZUMA COUNTY

Montezuma County was created from La Plata County in 1889 and named for the Aztec chief Moctezuma II. It is the location of Mesa Verde National Park, the Canyon of the Ancients and the Yucca House National Monument, as well as most of the Ute Mountain Indian Reservation, home of the Weeminuche Band of Utes.

Dolores

Dolores, named for the Dolores River, is the Spanish word for "sorrow." The town sits at the river's mouth, where its waters begin to flow north. Established as a station on the Rio Grande Southern Railroad, it replaced an earlier town, Big Bend, now submerged beneath the nearby McPhee Reservoir. Anasazi archaeological ruins are in proximity to Dolores, and it is also the home of Dunton Hot Springs Resort and Spa, set in a carefully restored ghost town (970-882-4800).

DOLORES HOTEL: Built before 1904, this hotel was operated by O.E. Puckett in 1904.
SOUTHERN HOTEL: Built before 1904, this hotel was operated by J.D. McGrew in 1904.

Mancos

Many have claimed Mancos, located between Durango and Cortez on U.S. 160, five miles east of the Mesa Verde National Park entrance. The town was founded in 1894, though ranchers began settling the Mancos Valley in the 1870s. Mancos, a stop on the Denver, Rio Grande and Southern Railway, was initially the main trade center for eastern Montezuma County, rivaling the town of Dolores. The area was once part of New Spain and Mexico, inhabited by Ute and Navajo, who contested for centuries over its control. It was part of the original Ute Reservation in 1868, but today the boundary of the Ute Mountain Indian Reservation is located six miles south of town. The name "Mancos" comes from the 1776 Dominguez-Escalante Expedition, though its meaning is unclear. At one point in the town, the expedition crossed the Rio Mancos, en route to California from Mexico. There are numerous pre-contact archaeological sites in the area; their residents are thought to have been those who withdrew to the cliff dwellings of Mesa Verde. In recent years, Durango has expanded to Mancos, and the town has become an art colony.

HOTEL LEMMON: Built before 1904, this hotel was operated by Mrs. L.M. Armstrong in 1904.
MANCOS HOUSE: Built before 1904, this hotel was operated by Mrs. Ella Ausburn in 1904.

Montrose County

Montrose was formed in 1883 from Gunnison County, following the Utes' removal from the Uncompahgre Valley. The county was named for its county seat of Montrose. In 1909, the Bureau of Reclamation completed the seven-mile-long Gunnison Tunnel, bringing irrigation water to the valley and markedly changing local agriculture.

Cimarron

Cimarron is set on the Cimarron River, twenty miles east of Montrose on U.S. Highway 50. Established in the 1880s as a railroad town with a station and roundhouse, it is today a quiet community providing access to Morrow Point Dam, fishing on Cimarron Creek and boating on Crystal Reservoir. The Denver and Rio Grande trestle, crossing the Cimarron River Gorge northeast of town, is on the National Register of Historic Places.

Black Cañon Hotel: Built before 1886, this hotel was operated by the Denver and Rio Grande Railway. A subsidiary of the Denver and Rio Grande, the Rio Grande Hotel Company, established the Black Cañon Hotel and Eating House in Cimarron, which became a popular stop.
Cimarron House: Built prior to 1904, this hotel was operated by Mrs. W.J. McNamara in 1904.

Montrose

Montrose was incorporated in 1882 after the Utes were moved to reservations in Utah. The town's founder, Joseph Selig, is believed to have chosen the name for Sir Walter Scott's *A Legend of Montrose*.

In 1905, the Uncompahgre National Forest was established to manage and protect wildlife resources. In 1909, the Gunnison Tunnel opened, delivering water from the Gunnison River to Uncompahgre Valley, transforming the semi-arid valley into an agricultural hub. Montrose is a favorite place for outdoor adventure, with five national forests, the Black Canyon of the Gunnison National Park and three ski areas.

Hotel Belvedere: Built before 1904, this hotel was operated by O.P. Maxfield in 1904.

MORSE'S LODGE: This hotel was built sometime in the 1920s.

SMITH CENTRAL HOTEL: Built before 1904, this hotel was operated by E.H. Smith in 1904.

OURAY COUNTY

Formed from San Juan County in 1877, Ouray County is named for Chief Ouray, distinguished chief of the Uncompahgre band of Utes. For his leadership abilities, he was recognized by whites as an important ally. Ouray was a peacemaker, seeking reconciliation between the races, as he understood that war with whites might mean the end of his people. For this stand, the more militant Utes thought him a coward. The Uncompahgre Utes did not participate in the infamous Meeker Massacre; rather, Chief Ouray helped to bring about an end to the bloodshed. Though he often dressed in the white man's clothing, Ouray never cut his long hair. In 1899, after meeting with the Ute leader in Washington, D.C., President Hayes described Ouray as the most intellectual man he had ever spoken with. Two different mountains are named in the Ute chief's honor: Mount Ouray in the Sawatch Range and Ouray Peak in Chaffee County. Due to its rugged mountain geography, Ouray County has been called the Switzerland of America.

Ouray

Centuries before the white man's arrival, the nomadic Tabeguache Utes traveled here in the summer to hunt and bathe in the sacred waters of the springs. The town was once called "Uncompahgre," a Ute word meaning "hot water springs." After respected Chief Ouray reluctantly signed the 1875 treaty relinquishing the Utes' beloved San Juan Mountains to whites, gold and silver seekers began pouring in. At one time, Ouray had more horses and mules than people, and at the peak of its mining heydays, it had over thirty mines. The town was incorporated in 1876 and named for Chief Ouray; its population rose to over one thousand when it became the county seat and saw the arrival of the Denver and Rio Grande Railway, all in one year. The whole town is registered as a National Historic District, and most of its buildings date to the late 1800s.

*BEAUMONT HOTEL: 505 Main Street, Ouray, CO 81427; 970-325-7000, 888-447-3255; beaumonthotel.com.

This hotel was first envisioned by a partnership of five leading citizens, who engaged architect Mr. O. Bulow to design it. The Beaumont, which means "beautiful mountain," opened in 1886 and was called the "Flagship of the San Juans." Cascade Falls and three towering mountains are the background for this magnificent example of late Victorian Gothic architecture. The thirty-thousand-square-foot building occupies half a block on the prominent corner of Fifth Avenue and Main Street.

During its colorful history, the Beaumont has been host to many famous guests, including actress Sarah Bernhardt, who performed from the balcony; Presidents Herbert Hoover and Theodore Roosevelt; Ute Chief Ouray and his wife, Chipeta; and King Leopold of Belgium.

The hotel spent its first seventy-five years under various owners and managers, but none so perverse as Wayland Phillips of Chicago, who purchased the hotel in 1964 and was turned down by the city when she requested a designated parking area. In a fit of pique, she closed the hotel, boarded it up, painted it pink and then left it to the elements for almost thirty-five years, until part of its roof collapsed. Upon Phillips's death, the Beaumont was in such disrepair that it was near to being razed. But in 1998, it was put up for auction and purchased by new owners, who hoped to restore its original grandeur.

The Beaumont, celebrating its handsome restoration in its 115th year. *Photo courtesy of the Beaumont Hotel.*

Local workers salvaged furnishings, reclaimed floors and ceilings, updated wiring and plumbing, removed the Beaumont's peeling pink outer skin and restored the brick and mortar. After five years of intensive restoration, the Beaumont once again opened to the public. A state-of-the-art spa now occupies the third floor, and the hotel's Grand Ballroom, with twenty-eight-foot ceilings and thirteen-foot-high stained-glass Romanesque windows, is an inspiring place for every possible celebration and event.

The hotel is home to Bulow's Bistro (honoring the architect), offering a casual lunch and dinner menu in the secluded, European setting of the courtyard. The second-floor Voodoo Lounge, serving cocktails and appetizers, overlooks the courtyard and surrounding mountains.

The Beaumont is listed on the National Register of Historic Places and was the 2003 recipient of the National Preservation Award, the State of Colorado 2003 Governor's Award for Historic Preservation and the 2004 Preserve America Presidential Award. Today, the magnificent Beaumont, the intrepid Flagship of the San Juans, is still welcoming guests from all over the globe.

*ST. ELMO HOTEL: 426 Main Street, Ouray, CO 81427; 970-325-4951; stelmohotel.com.

The St. Elmo Hotel, circa 1898.

The Western Hotel, one of the oldest buildings in the state and still in operation. *Photo courtesy of the Western Hotel.*

The St. Elmo Hotel was built in 1898 by Kittie O'Brien (later Heit), primarily as a miners' hotel during the gold and silver boom in the San Juan Mountains. The hotel was located next door to her Bon Ton Restaurant, which began operating about 1886. O'Brien, an attractive, capable woman with an entrepreneurial spirit, came to Ouray in 1886 with her son Freddy, then twelve. In 1889, Kittie married electrician Joseph Heit, and in 1903, they adopted a boy, Francis. In 1893, following the silver crash, when many lost their jobs, Kittie offered free sleeping rooms to miners, making her a beloved local figure.

Freddy began living a dissolute life of gambling and violence, while Francis enlisted during World War I. Sadly, Kittie died of a heart attack, and for a time, Freddie ran the St. Elmo. But when he put the hotel up as collateral for a gambling debt, the hotel was auctioned off. Freddie then shot himself, and his wife somehow acquired the hotel. She transferred it to Francis in 1920. Three years later, Francis sold the hotel, and it changed hands a number of times over the years until the current owners purchased it.

The St. Elmo Hotel is listed on the National Register of Historic Places as part of the National Historical District of Ouray, Colorado. It has been restored into a nine-room Victorian inn, with antique furnishings in guest rooms and common areas, many of them original to the property.

The hotel's award-winning Bon Ton Restaurant offers specialties in Italian fare, prime Angus steaks, beef Wellington, rack of lamb and fresh seafood. It has an outstanding wine list and martini bar. Now located downstairs in the St. Elmo Hotel, the restaurant is decorated with rock walls, hardwood floors and a beautiful bar.

*WESTERN HOTEL: 210 Seventh Avenue, Ouray, CO 81427; 970-325-4645, 888-624-8403; historicwesternhotel.com.

Built in 1892 by John Johnstone and Fred Mayol, the Western Hotel is one of the largest frame buildings on the western slope. The Victorian Italianate structure has its original high tin ceilings, stained glass, historic bar and lobby. Rooms are updated with private baths but retain period furnishings.

The hotel has hosted the spectacular San Juan Scenic Jeep Tour since 1946 and features a saloon and restaurant, serving lunch and dinner.

WILSON HOTEL: Built before 1904, this hotel was operated by G.H. Wilson in 1904.

Ridgway

Named for railroad superintendent Robert M. Ridgway, this town was established in 1891. It is the northern entrance of the scenic San Juan Skyway. Located in the unspoiled Uncompahgre Valley, surrounded by the snow-capped Cimarron and San Juan Mountains, Ridgway is called the "Gateway to the San Juans." This lofty position was established when the Rio Grande Southern made Ridgway a railhead center to service the mining towns of Ouray and Telluride. To preserve the town's railroad history, the

Ridgway Railroad Museum is located at the junction of U.S. Highway 550 and Colorado State Highway 62.

The region's scenery and considerable wildlife make it a photographer's paradise, with indigenous mountain lion, badger, deer, elk, bear, coyote and wild turkey. Bald eagles nest in century-old cottonwoods along the river in late fall, and the Ridgway Town Park offers picnicking. Ridgway's park and the surrounding areas were locations for the movies *How the West Was Won* and John Wayne's *True Grit.*

LA VETA HOUSE: Built before 1904, this hotel was operated by Mrs. H. Lynch in 1904.
MENTONE HOTEL: Built before 1904, this hotel was operated by P.F. Brockway in 1904.

RIO BLANCO COUNTY

Rio Blanco County was created in 1889 from Summit County. The county is named in the Spanish language for the White River, which runs through it.

Meeker

A terrible massacre also bears the name of this town. In 1878, Nathan Meeker, founder of Greeley, Colorado, was appointed Indian agent at the White River Indian Reserve. He believed he owed Horace Greeley a debt and sought the agency job to repay his old mentor. Meeker's actions would bring disaster. His contact with Indians was minimal, and he was insensitive to Ute culture. He moved the agency eleven miles down the White River to Powell Park, three miles from present-day Meeker. Both the move and Meeker's ideas were unpopular with the Indians, who pastured large herds of ponies in the meadows of Powell Park. To prove their value as Indian men, they would race the ponies and hunt with them to feed their families. Meeker believed the ponies were major obstacles to his intentions of making the Utes into farmers, so he decided to plow up their racetrack.

His plan was met with outrage from the Utes, so Meeker asked for troops to protect the agency. When the government finally sent Major Thornburg and troops from Fort Steele, this served to further enrage the Indians, who did not appreciate soldiers on their reservation. A battle ensued between the Utes and the army at Milk Creek. Reinforcements in the form of Captain

Dodge and his few Buffalo Soldiers arrived later. One Buffalo Soldier, Sergeant Henry Johnson, distinguished himself in the rescue by obtaining water for the wounded from Milk Creek, at great risk to himself. He was the first black man to receive the Congressional Medal of Honor and is buried at Arlington National Cemetery.

But the Utes also attacked the Indian agency. By ignoring warnings from knowledgeable ranchers, as well as direct warnings from the Utes, Meeker doomed the agency men and himself. White River Utes killed them all, burned the agency and captured the women and children. The Utes did not want to surrender their captives, but Chief Ouray's sister, Susan, convinced them to do so, and the women and children were released after twenty-three days. Despite his unfortunate choices, Nathan Meeker is honored by the town's bearing his name.

Following the 1879 massacre, the army moved to the present site of Meeker, where it established a permanent military camp with barracks, barns, officers' quarters and other buildings. In 1883, the government auctioned off all its buildings to settlers, and the town was incorporated in 1885. In 1900, Theodore Roosevelt, then governor of New York and vice president elect, stayed at the Meeker Hotel, which became the starting point of his hunt for mountain lions. Meeker is the Rio Blanco County seat.

The first Meeker Hotel, a converted adobe army barracks, circa 1884–85.

Reuben Sanford Ball, owner and proprietor, sits at a table in the lobby of the new Meeker Hotel, sometime between 1896 and 1910. The hotel was noted for its unique foyer, with relics of many hunts.

*MEEKER HOTEL: 560 Main Street, Meeker, CO 81641; 970-878-5255; themeekerhotel.com.

A partnership between Charlie Dunbar and Susan Wright established the Meeker Hotel sometime before 1884, but Dunbar was shot and killed over a card game only months after the hotel and café opened. Wright is acknowledged as one of Meeker's town founders. Rueben Sanford Ball, Wright's brother, went to work for his sister in 1891. When Susan Wright died of illness in 1893, she willed the property to her brother. Under Ball's ownership, the new Meeker Hotel and Café was constructed in 1896 on the site of the present historic Meeker Hotel. In 1904, east and west wings were added. The stone building, currently housing the Meeker Café, was, in 1891, Meeker's new post office, and in 1904, it became the First National Bank Building. In 1918, Ball moved the café from the hotel to the stone building.

SAN JUAN COUNTY

This county's river and surrounding mountain range were named for Saint John by early Spanish explorers. Silverton is the county's only municipality and is the county seat.

Silverton

When the Brunot Treaty opened the San Juan valley for settlement in 1873, settlers streamed in for various purposes. Many were drawn by gold and silver. Some sought to escape their pasts, while others hoped to earn money to send home to families. Seeking cheap labor, mining companies advertised overseas, promising jobs and opportunities to become landowners. In the mid-1880s, large numbers came from Austria, Italy, Serbia, Croatia, Cornwall, Ireland, Wales, France, Germany, Russia, Norway, Sweden and Denmark. These hopefuls made the exhausting ocean voyage in unpleasant conditions, only to arrive in America and have to cross the continent to reach Silverton. Very few spoke English.

Set in the San Juan Mountains, at an elevation of 9,318 feet, in its heyday, Silverton boasted twenty-seven saloons and two bona fide hotels that were not brothels. Rooms were hard to find, liquor flowed like rivers and the town was anything but quiet. The town's name describes its major resource: "Silver by the Ton." A typical mining camp, Silverton was rife with bordellos, gambling dens and dance halls. And according to one 1884 local newspaper article, Silverton also swarmed with dogs, which invaded hotels and came to meals with their masters. The dogs fought publicly amongst themselves, mirroring human activity in the bars and streets.

But times change, and so has Silverton. It is now a quaint mountain town with a colorful history, vivid memories and some lively—and likely lurid—tales to whisper of its past.

The Durango and Silverton Narrow Gauge Railroad operates forty-five miles of track between the two towns. In 1882, the rails from Durango to Silverton were completed, and although the line had been initially constructed to haul gold and silver ore from the San Juan Mountains, the train soon began hauling both freight and passengers, who sought the dramatic views. The historic train has been in continuous operation for 128 years. Though it's now a tourist and heritage line, it is one of the few still carrying passengers behind vintage steam locomotives on rolling stock original to the line.

COMMERCIAL HOUSE: This hotel was built sometime in the 1890s.

THE COTTON HOUSE: This house was built before 1883.

GOLD KING HOTEL: This hotel was built between 1870 and 1890, near Silverton in San Juan County.

*GRAND IMPERIAL HOTEL: 1219 Greene Street, Silverton, CO 81433; 970-387-5527, 800-341-3340; grandimperialhotel.com.

This hotel was built in 1882 by W.S. Thompson, an Englishman, and his partner, Dr. S.H. Beckwith, and designed by a French architect. Thompson, who owned interest in a local smelter, elegantly fitted out his new hotel with fine carpets and marble-topped furniture. Its second floor held eighteen generous rooms, with thirty-eight more on the third floor. The hotel's bar, originally the Hub Saloon, located in the lobby, became the favored watering hole of the silver kings, boasting that it never shut its doors. The hotel still has its beautiful bar with a bullet hole in it, a souvenir of Silverton's wilder days, though its source is not clearly remembered. The favored tale is that the bullet hole was made by Bat Masterson while attempting to arrest someone. Of course, Masterson's trusty sidekicks, Wyatt Earp and Doc Holliday, also hung out at the saloon with him, so the door to speculation is wide open.

The saloon's mirrors came from France and are nearly an inch thick; no one has shot them yet. The bar itself was one of three pieces made in England. Its two end pieces are still in use, one in Telluride and the other located in Tombstone, Arizona.

The Grand Imperial's early clientele drew from the roster of silver barons and railroad magnates. Since the Grand Imperial's saloon was on the respectable side of the street, it remained relatively free of the moral stigma attached to its neighbors. But across the street from the hotel was the "liquor side" of town, as nine out of twelve city lots held saloons. One street over from the Grand Imperial was the notorious Blair Street, Silverton's red-light district. There is rumor of a tunnel beneath the Grand Imperial leading to Blair Street, but it has not been verified. The reported tunnel would allow gentlemen staying at the hotel to come in the front entrance with respectable ladies and step out through the tunnel for brandy and cigars—or whatever—getting back before anyone was the wiser.

Before the advent of indoor plumbing, the hotel's third floor was rented as guest rooms, and water for the rooms had to be hauled in from Anvil Mountain, located behind the hotel. The second floor was utilized as offices for doctors, lawyers, the town hall and the post office.

But Prohibition cut drastically into the Grand Imperial's finances, and for years the hotel struggled, on the brink of closing. In the 1950s, it was rescued and renovated, presenting a fresh face and forty rooms with private baths for visiting tourists.

In 1956, Barbara Stanwyck starred in the movie *The Maverick Queen*, filmed in the Grand Imperial. The hotel also has its share of ghost stories. There was a fellow named Luigi, a doctor apparently unable to cure his own broken heart. He was staying in Room 28 when he shot himself in 1890. The poor

A postcard of the Grand Imperial Hotel. In 1904, it was operated by C.L. Petherbridge.

man was reportedly tormented, possibly over a Blair Street woman. He has since been seen in a top hat, leaning over the beds of guests as they sleep, as if checking in on patients.

Today, the hotel is home to Grumpy's Saloon and Restaurant, which offers a varied menu, including excellent chili and world-famous French onion soup, with a live honky-tonk piano on the side. It is open year-round, serving breakfast, lunch and dinner, and has a full bar with microbrews on tap.

Sitting proudly on the main street of town, close to the terminus of the scenic railroad, the hotel is a gem cradled in the San Juan Mountains. A tenacious survivor, this mansard-roofed granite structure maintains its elaborate fourteen-foot ceilings, ornate chandeliers and, of course, its ghosts. The Grand Imperial is still welcoming guests today.

THE MELTON: This hotel was built before 1904.
THE SILVERTON HOTEL: This hotel was built before 1883.
WALKER HOUSE: This hotel was built before 1883.

SAN MIGUEL COUNTY

This county was created in 1883, and given the Spanish name of Saint Michael for the nearby San Miguel River. The area is known for its stunning mountain scenery, mining history and the town of Telluride, the county seat, famous for its world-class ski resorts.

Ames: Ghost Town

Ames began in 1880 when Otto Mears built a toll road connecting Telluride and Ouray. He used this location as a stage stop and post office, but the railroad did not pass nearby. Ames might have simply faded into oblivion but for one Lucien L. Nunn from Ohio. In 1890, this short-lived, now-forgotten town near Ophir made history as the first place that commercial alternating current (AC) electricity was extensively used in mining. Ames is located below the Gold King Mine at twelve thousand feet. Its power plant was the creation of Nunn, who was lured west by the Colorado mining boom. Nunn was an admirer of Nikola Tesla, developer of AC, a form of electric power that could be transmitted across long distances with less loss of energy than direct current.

Nunn had practiced law, and by 1888, he bought control of the San Miguel County Bank, which was robbed by Butch Cassidy and the Sundance Kid the next year. Nunn persuaded principal stockholders of the Gold King Mine to back AC current, and he then managed to meet with Westinghouse and convince him to invest in his venture using AC current. Westinghouse bought patents from Tesla to build AC generators

Ames Hotel, circa 1880s.

and motors, costing $1 million. Nunn became manager of the Gold King, recruiting his brother, Paul, to help design the Ames Power Plant. Students from Cornell University and locals were hired for construction of the facility. Water flumes built from local creeks above the power plant provided elevation that ran the generator. In June 1891, the Nunns unleashed water from Howard and Lake, tributaries of the San Miguel's South Fork below the mine, to a big wheel belted to a generator. Once the power plant was completed, lines were strung to the mine, and electricity was transmitted two and a half miles over rugged terrain to a motor-driven mill at Gold King. This cut down on the expense of fuel, and after the Nunns' success with this experimental technology, power lines were soon strung to mines throughout the region.

From his successful Ames venture, Lucien Nunn would become highly respected in the field of power generation, helping to build the first Canadian AC hydroelectric power plant at Niagara Falls. Public Service Co. acquired the Ames plant in 1992 in a bankruptcy proceeding. The original wood structure housing the water wheel has been replaced by a granite building, and according to the plant's operators, if properly maintained, the Ames plant could run for another hundred years.

AMES HOTEL: This hotel was built before 1880.

Norwood

This town is built on top of Wrights Mesa. There were no white settlers until 1879, when Edwin Joseph first homesteaded the area. Norwood was eventually a ranching community, and when mining was introduced, the town became a significant supply town. Norwood is today known for its cattle ranches and is a destination for outdoor enthusiasts.

NORWOOD HOTEL: This hotel was built before 1898 on Main Street.

Ophir

Named after an Arabian city rich in gold, Ophir was born in 1875 when gold was discovered in the area. It is located a few miles from the site of the world's first commercial system to generate and transmit alternating current electricity: the Ames Hydroelectric Plant.

HOTEL ELLIOTT: Built before 1904, this hotel was operated by Mrs. Martin Hisey in 1904.

OPHIR HOTEL: This hotel was built before 1920.

SILVER MOUNTAIN HOTEL: Built before 1890, this hotel was operated by Mrs. Ella H. Dinan in 1904.

VICTOR HOTEL: Built before 1904, this hotel was operated by Mrs. G. Willis in 1904.

WOODSON HOUSE: Built before 1904, this hotel was operated by Mrs. A.W. Woodson in 1904.

Placerville

The town was originally a small mining camp named for placer gold mines on the San Miguel River and Leopard Creek. Its original location became known as Old Placerville, after the Rio Grande Southern Railroad built a depot and sidings west of town, calling the new area Placerville.

In the 1890s, A.B. Frenzel discovered vanadium ore in the sandstone east of Placerville. Although of inferior grade, a determined Frenzel drove one tunnel eighteen feet into rock, and by 1901–02, he was excavating thousands of tons meant for Europe. But as the ore was too low grade to justify shipment cost, in 1905 the Vanadium Alloys Co. built an ore-processing mill southeast of Placerville to recover ferrovanadium, which it sold. Frenzel, not a man to easily give up, was justified.

20TH CENTURY HOUSE: Built before 1904, this hotel was operated by Mrs. E.E. Elliot & Son in 1904.

Telluride

At 8,750 feet of elevation, Telluride nestles in a box canyon in an isolated spot in the Four Corners region, where Colorado, New Mexico, Utah and Arizona join. Steep mountains and cliffs surround the town, with Bridal Veil Falls at the head of the canyon. It was once a summer camp for the Ute Indians until the San Juan Mountains lured fortune hunters with promises of silver and gold. About 1875, the Sheridan Mine was the first of numerous local claims. Initially a tent city first called Columbia, the mining camp became a town in 1878, changing its name to Telluride. The town takes its name from an element called Tellurium, a metalloid associated with gold and silver deposits—although Tellurium was never found in the area.

With the railroad's arrival in 1890, the remote town prospered. Immigrants seeking fortunes turned Telluride into a community of five thousand, until the silver crash of 1893, followed by World War I. Miners moved on, and the town's population dwindled to hundreds. But in the 1970s, Telluride made a new discovery—powder snow, as good as gold! That started a new boom, and when the Telluride Ski Resort opened in 1973, the town's renaissance began. A free gondola connects the town with its neighbor, Mountain Village, at the base of the ski area. The Telluride Historic District includes a significant part of town and is listed on the National Register of Historic Places. It is also one of Colorado's twenty National Historic Landmarks.

THE NEW COLORADO HOUSE: Built in 1899, this hotel was gone by 1910.
*NEW SHERIDAN HOTEL: 231 West Colorado Avenue, Telluride, CO 81435; 970-728-4351, 800-200-1891; newsheridan.com.

The New Sheridan was built in 1895. As Telluride grew, so did its need for lodging. Like the town itself, the hotel was built with riches from gold and silver strikes in the surrounding San Juan Mountains.

The original Sheridan Hotel was a three-story frame structure, built at 233 West Colorado Avenue, east of the courthouse. In 1894, the original building was destroyed by fire. The present brick building at 231 West Colorado Avenue was erected next door to the burned lot, opening in 1895 as the New Sheridan Hotel (the Sheridan has remained "new" ever since). L.L. Nunn, Ames power plant genius, was instrumental in bringing AC electric power to Telluride, and the hotel has been lit by electricity from its beginning.

In 1899, a two-story brick addition was built on the site of the original hotel, but for a second time it was destroyed by fire. No more attempts were made to build on the original lot for nearly a century; the land appears in historic photos as a grassy yard. It was not until 1994 that a two-story building housing the New Sheridan Restaurant, additional hotel rooms and a sun deck above was constructed there. In 1994, the hotel also underwent a metamorphosis from a miners' hotel to twenty-six luxury hotel rooms and suites, complete with Victorian antiques.

In the 1890s, the hotel was the town's social center. Its Continental Room Restaurant held sixteen velvet-curtained booths, each equipped with a button to discreetly summon a waiter when needed. Its adjoining American Room was said to have rivaled the Brown Palace in Denver in service and cuisine. It has been reported that in those days, it was possible for a man to

The New Sheridan today. Beautifully restored, the hotel and its fine restaurant are still welcoming skiers and tourists to the historic heart of Telluride. *Photo courtesy of the New Sheridan Hotel.*

enjoy dinner with his mistress in the Continental Room and his wife in the American Room, at the same time—though why any man would find such stress enjoyable is hard to imagine.

Music was discreetly hidden behind doors near the ceiling (still evident), where a small trio or quartet could be seated in the mezzanine of the bar. With the doors opened out, musicians could play for guests of both dining rooms and the bar simultaneously.

For a brief period early in the 1900s, the New Sheridan Bar was converted into a grocery store (H.H. Walrod & Co. Grocers) and was boycotted by local miners during labor disputes. The hotel, bar and restaurants were then owned by the Sheridan Mines Company. After labor issues were settled, the old saloon reverted back to its proper function. During Prohibition, liquor service was curtailed but not entirely terminated. The New Sheridan Bar, the town's oldest, remains much as it was in 1895, with a handsomely carved mahogany bar from Austria, room dividers of leaded and beveled glass panels and ornate light fixtures.

The New Sheridan is home to the world-renowned restaurant The Chop House and the Parlor Bar, both offering fine foods, rich history and superior service. The New Sheridan Hotel has been welcoming guests for over one hundred years and is just getting started.

Sᴀɴ Jᴜᴀɴ Hᴏᴛᴇʟ: This hotel was built sometime before 1904.

Vɪᴄᴛᴏʀɪᴀ Hᴏᴛᴇʟ: Built before 1904, this hotel was operated by J.E. Marchland in 1904.

Appendix A

RECIPES FROM THE
KITCHENS OF COLORADO'S
HISTORIC HOTELS

THE BROADMOOR'S TAVERN RESTAURANT

Oysters Rockefeller

Yield: 4 servings

This dish was invented at Antoine's about 1900 and named for Rockefeller because it was incredibly rich. It is simple to prepare at home, and any extra sauce can be shaped and refrigerated. Use the freshest shucked oysters you can obtain, and ask for the deeper half of the shell. Oysters on half shells on rock salt is the classic presentation. You can also use small scallop shells or ramekins.

2 dozen oysters on the half shell, drained
4 pans rock salt
1 cup salted butter, softened
1 cup cooked spinach, finely chopped
¼ cup fresh parsley, finely chopped
½ cup scallions, finely chopped
¾ teaspoon salt
½ teaspoon ground white pepper

$\frac{1}{2}$ teaspoon dried marjoram
$\frac{1}{2}$ teaspoon dried basil
$\frac{1}{2}$ teaspoon cayenne
$\frac{1}{4}$ cup Pernod

Combine all ingredients in a stainless steel or ceramic bowl and cream with a wooden spoon. Complete mixing with a whisk or electric beater at medium speed. Shape the sauce into oval patties about 2 $\frac{1}{2}$ by 2 inches and $\frac{1}{2}$-inch thick by scooping 2 tablespoons of sauce from the bowl with your fingers and pressing into the palm of your hand. Set the patties on a platter and refrigerate while preparing the oysters for baking. Preheat oven to 500 degrees Fahrenheit. Wash oyster shells thoroughly and dry. Place a drained oyster on each shell and set 6 to a pan on rock salt. Cover each oyster with a patty of sauce and bake 14 to 16 minutes, until the sauce bubbles and becomes lightly browned on top. Set pans on serving plates and allow to cool for 3 to 6 minutes before serving.

Variation: Many restaurants place hollandaise on top before serving.

Hollandaise Sauce

Yield: 20 ounces

2 ounces cider vinegar
$\frac{1}{2}$ teaspoon whole black peppercorns, fresh cracked
4 ounces water
6 each egg yolks
12 ounces clarified butter, warm
2 teaspoons lemon juice
Salt and pepper to taste

Combine vinegar and peppercorns; reduce until the liquid has almost cooked away. Cool the reduction slightly and strain. Add hot water to strained reduction. Add the reduction to the egg yolks. In a stainless steel bowl, whip over simmering water until the yolks ribbon and triple in volume. They should have a light but firm consistency. Gradually add the warm clarified butter, whipping constantly. Add the lemon juice and adjust seasoning to taste with salt and pepper.

Blintz Souffle

FILLING
8 ounces cream cheese
2 cups ricotta cheese
2 egg yolks
1 tablespoon sugar
1 teaspoon vanilla

BATTER
1/2 cup softened butter
1/3 cup sugar
Eggs, plus 2 egg whites
1 cup flour
1 teaspoon baking powder
1 1/2 cup sour cream
1 cup orange juice

In a small bowl, beat cream cheese until smooth. Add remaining filling ingredients and mix thoroughly.

In a large bowl mix flour and baking powder, set aside.

In a greased 9 x 13 pan, spread half the batter. Layer with the filling, followed by the remainder of the batter. Bake at 350 degrees Fahrenheit for about an hour, until a knife inserted comes out clean. Let stand 10 minutes before cutting into 8 to 10 servings. This casserole may be served immediately or cooked one day ahead and served after reheating. To serve, garnish with a sauce made by heating a favorite jam and add complimentary fruits. For example, with a chunky peach jam, add pitted black cherries.

Brown Palace Hotel, Denver

Afternoon Tea

Executive Pastry Chef David Lewis

Sundried Tomato and Swiss Scones

4 cups all-purpose flour
$\frac{1}{2}$ cup sugar, granulated
1 tablespoon baking powder
2 teaspoons baking soda
1 teaspoon salt, iodized
$1\frac{1}{2}$ cups butter
2 cups buttermilk
$\frac{3}{4}$ cup cubed Swiss cheese
$\frac{3}{4}$ cup sun-dried tomatoes

Mix all dry ingredients together by hand. Mix in buttermilk and melted butter, DO NOT OVERMIX. Mix in cheese and tomatoes. Put in a rectangle baking dish flat and refrigerate for 2 hours. Cut into desired shape, separate and bake on cookie sheet at 350 Fahrenheit until golden brown, about 16 minutes.

Brown Palace Ship Tavern

Executive Chef Bill Dexter

Seafood Chowder

$\frac{1}{2}$ bacon fat/butter
$\frac{1}{4}$ cup chopped bacon (1 slice)
$\frac{1}{2}$ pound onions
$\frac{1}{2}$ pound celery
1 tablespoon garlic

1 1/2 cups flour
3 cups clam juice
1/2 each bay leaf
1/8 teaspoon cayenne pepper
1 teaspoon thyme
1 pound diced potatoes
3 cups milk
3 cups chopped clams
Desired poached seafood
Salt and pepper to taste
1/2 ounces Sherry wine
Parsley, chopped
Steamed manila clam

In medium 6-quart stockpot, heat bacon fat to medium temperature, add bacon, onion, celery and garlic and sweat until translucent (approx 4 to 5 minutes). Add flour and cook an additional 5 to 8 minutes. Add clam juice, bay leaf, cayenne and thyme and simmer on low heat for 10 minutes. Add potatoes and milk and simmer for 15 minutes. Add clams and poached fish as desired and season with salt and pepper to taste. Thin with water if needed and garnish with 1/2 ounces of sherry wine and chopped parsley and a steamed manila clam.

Palace Arms Restaurant

Executive Sous Chef Thanawat Bates

Pan-Seared Crab Cakes with Coconut Lemongrass Froth

1/3 cup mayonnaise
1 whole egg
1 tablespoon of Dijon mustard
2 teaspoons Old Bay™ seasoning
2 lemons
Salt and pepper to taste
1 pound jumbo lump crabmeat
1 diced skinless granny smith apple

1 bunch cilantro
1 red bell pepper
1 yellow bell pepper
3 stalks scallions
Panko™ breadcrumbs

In a mixing bowl, add mayonnaise, egg, Dijon mustard, Old Bay™ seasoning, lemon juice, salt and pepper. Taste mixture for correct seasoning. In separate mixing bowl, add crabmeat, apples, chopped cilantro, small diced red and yellow bell peppers, chopped scallion and breadcrumbs. Combine wet and dry mixtures into one bowl. Start molding your crab cakes into desired size. (If too wet, add more breadcrumbs.) Sear cake in a sauté pan with a little vegetable oil and butter until golden brown. Finish in a 350-degree oven until it reaches an internal temperature of 160 degrees.

COCONUT LEMONGRASS FROTH

1 pound lemongrass
4 whole shallots
5 cloves garlic
1 tablespoon fresh ginger
1 cup white wine
1 cup chicken stock
2 cups coconut milk
4 tablespoons tom ka paste (available at any Asian market)
½ bunch cilantro
½ bunch basil
2 tablespoons fresh mint
4 stocks of scallion
2 tablespoons chili flakes
Fish sauce to taste
Lime juice to taste

In a medium saucepot, sauté lemongrass, shallots, garlic and ginger for 5 to 10 minutes. Deglaze with white wine. Reduce to four tablespoons of liquid. Add 1 cup chicken stock and 2 cups coconut milk. Let it reduce by half. Add tom ka paste and then add cilantro, basil, mint, scallion and chili flakes. Let simmer for approximately 15 minutes to extract flavor and aromatic. Season with fish sauce and lime juice to taste. Strain to sauce. Ready to serve.

CALLAWAY'S AT THE DELAWARE HOTEL, LEADVILLE

Chicken Enchilada Soup

Yield: Serves 8 to 10

1 tablespoon vegetable oil
3 chicken breasts, cubed
½ cup diced onion
1 tablespoon minced garlic
4 cups chicken broth
1 cup flour
3 cups water
1 cup enchilada sauce
16 ounces Velveeta cheese
1 teaspoon salt
1 teaspoon chili powder
½ teaspoon cumin

1. Add 1 tablespoon oil to a stockpot over medium heat. Add the chicken and brown 5 minutes each side. Set chicken aside.
2. Add onions and garlic to stockpot and sauté over medium heat for 3 minutes or until onions are cooked through. Add chicken broth.
3. Mix flour with 2 cups water until blended. Add to onion/garlic/broth mixture.
4. Add rest of the water, enchilada sauce, cheese and spices to the pot and bring to a boil.
5. Add the chicken and cook for 30 minutes, until the stock is thick.
6. Serve garnished with shredded cheese and crumbled tortilla chips.

Shrimp and Watermelon Salad

Yield: Serves 6 to 8

2 tablespoons olive oil
1 pound peeled, deveined medium shrimp
2 teaspoons snipped fresh thyme
4 cups sliced bok choy or Napa cabbage

1 cup grape tomatoes, halved
Salt and pepper to taste
2 1-inch sliced seedless watermelon, halved
1 small lime, halved
Feta cheese
Fresh thyme sprigs

Heat 1 tablespoon oil in a large skillet over medium high heat. Add shrimp. Cook and stir 3 to 4 minutes until shrimp are opaque. Transfer shrimp to a bowl. Stir in thyme. Add remaining olive oil, bok choy and tomatoes to skillet. Cook and stir for 1 minute. Return shrimp to skillet. Cook and stir 1 more minute. Season with salt and pepper.

Serve shrimp and vegetables with watermelon. Squeeze lime juice on salad. Sprinkle on feta and thyme springs.

Conejos River Guest Ranch, Antonito

Tomato Dill Soup

¹/₂ cup butter
1 cup finely chopped carrots
1 cup finely chopped celery
1 cup finely chopped onions
2 teaspoons minced garlic
1 teaspoon basil
1 teaspoon thyme
1 teaspoon tarragon
¹/₂ cup flour
3 cups chicken broth
1 35-ounce can diced tomatoes
2¹/₂ cups tomato juice
1 cup heavy cream
1 teaspoon sugar
1 tablespoon dill weed
Fresh dill for garnish

Sauté carrots, celery and onion in butter for 8 to 10 minutes. Stir in garlic and other spices. Cook for 1 minutes. Stir in flour and cook for 4 to 5 minutes. Add chicken broth, tomatoes and juice. Boil, reduce heat and simmer for 10 minutes. Stir in cream and sugar and cook 5 minutes, or until thoroughly heated. Just before serving, add dill weed. Garnish with fresh dill on top of each serving.

White Chocolate Cheesecake

1 cup crushed shortbread cookies
3 tablespoon finely chopped toasted almonds
¹/₄ cup melted margarine or butter
2 8-ounce packages softened cream cheese
2 6-ounce package white chocolate baking bars, melted and cooled

$^2/_3$ cup sugar
3 eggs
$^2/_3$ cup sour cream
1 teaspoon vanilla
1 10-ounce jar strawberry preserves
1 cup fresh or frozen strawberries, sliced
Whole strawberries and/or mint sprigs for garnish

Combine crushed cookies and chopped almonds in small mixing bowl. Stir in melted butter or margarine. Press mixture evenly onto bottom of an 8-inch springform pan. Set aside. Beat cream cheese and prepared baking bars in large mixing bowl with electric mixer on medium high until combined. Add sugar, beating until mixture is smooth. Add eggs, sour cream and vanilla. Beat on low until combined. Do not overbeat. Pour filling into crust-lined pan. Place pan on shallow baking pan in oven and bake at 350 degrees Fahrenheit for 45 minutes, until center appears nearly set when gently shaken.

Do not over bake. This cheesecake puffs up during baking and then settles as it cools. Remove springform pan from oven and cool cheesecake on wire rack for 15 minutes. Use a small metal spatula to loosen sides of cheesecake from pan. Cool for 30 minutes more. Remove side of springform pan. Cool for an hour. Cover and chill for at least 4 hours.

Melt preserves in a small saucepan over low heat. Add strawberries. Heat gently, just until sauce simmers, and then cool. To serve, cut cheesecake into wedges, drizzle strawberry sauce over each serving and garnish.

Double Coconut Cream Pie

Shorty Fry, Conejos River Ranch "Pie-Master" recommends this one!

3 beaten egg yolks
$^1/_3$ cup sugar
$^1/_4$ cup cornstarch
$^1/_4$ teaspoon salt
2 cups milk
1 8-ounce can of cream of coconut ($^3/_4$ cup; not coconut milk)
2 tablespoons butter or margarine
1 cup flaked coconut

2 teaspoons vanilla
1 baked piecrust

MERINGUE
4 egg whites
$^1/_4$ teaspoon cream of tartar
$^1/_2$ teaspoon vanilla
$^1/_3$ cup sugar
Flaked coconut

Let egg whites stand at room temperature for 30 minutes. Meanwhile, combine $^1/_3$ cup sugar, cornstarch and salt in medium saucepan. Stir in milk and cream of coconut. Cook and stir over medium heat until thickened and bubbly, and then cook and stir 2 minutes more. Gradually stir about 1 cup of the hot milk mixture into beaten egg yolks, stirring constantly. Return all of the mixture to saucepan. Cook and stir until bubbly and then cook and stir 2 minutes more. Remove from heat. Stir in butter or margarine until melted. Stir in coconut and 2 teaspoons vanilla. Pour filling into baked pastry shell.

For meringue, beat 4 egg whites, $^1/_4$ teaspoon cream of tartar and $^1/_2$ teaspoon vanilla until soft peaks form. Gradually beat in $^1/_3$ cup sugar, 1 tablespoon at a time, until stiff. Spread over hot filling and seal at pastry edge. Sprinkle with flaked coconut. Bake at 350 degrees Fahrenheit for 15 minutes, or until lightly browned.

Recipes from the Kitchens of Colorado's Historic Hotels

Eastholme in the Rockies B&B, Cascade

Amish Breakfast Casserole

Yield: Serves 8 to 10

1 pound sliced bacon, diced
1 medium sweet onion
6 eggs, lightly beaten
4 cups frozen shredded hash brown potatoes
2 cups shredded mild cheddar cheese
1 1/2 cups small curd cottage cheese
1 1/4 cups shredded Swiss cheese

In a large skillet, cook bacon and onion until bacon is crisp, then drain. Mix together remaining ingredients and stir in bacon mixture. Transfer to greased 9 x 13 pan. Bake, uncovered, at 350 degrees Fahrenheit for 35 to 40 minutes or until eggs are set and bubbly. Let stand 10 minutes before serving.

Artichoke Baked Omelet

Yield: Serves 8 to 10

1 1/2 cups hot or mild salsa
1 cup chopped marinated artichoke hearts
2/3 cups grated Parmesan cheese
1 1/2 cups shredded Monterey Jack cheese
1 1/2 cups shredded cheddar cheese
10 eggs (beaten)
8 ounces sour cream

Preheat oven to 350 degrees Fahrenheit. In bottom of a 9 x 13 glass baking dish (sprayed with Pam), layer salsa, artichoke hearts, parmesan cheese, Monterey jack cheese and cheddar cheese.

In a large bowl, whisk together eggs and sour cream until smooth. Pour egg/sour cream mixture over cheese mixture. Bake uncovered for 1 hour or until lightly brown and egg is set.

FRISCO LODGE, BRECKENRIDGE

Belgian Waffles

1 cup flour
3 tablespoons melted butter
1 cup sour cream
2 tablespoons sugar
$^1/_2$ teaspoon salt
1 egg yolk
$^1/_2$ cup milk
1 egg white, stiffly beaten

Mix together all ingredients. Gently stir in beaten egg white after all other ingredients are thoroughly mixed. Bake in a heated waffle iron 2 to 3 minutes or slightly longer. Serve with desired topping.

The Peck House, Empire

Loin of Lamb

Yield: Serves 8

Grill the loin of lamb to medium rare, taking care not to overcook. Lamb chops may be substituted. Cover with following sauce and serve.

Plum Sauce

8 ripe dark plums
½ cup sugar
¼ cup port wine
1 teaspoon crushed dried mint

Pit the plums and slice them thin. Add all ingredients to a saucepan and simmer over medium heat until thick and bubbly. Serve with any grilled red meat or lamb.

Peck House Sour Cream Coffee Cake

6 eggs
1½ cup oil
3 cups sour cream or yogurt
1 tablespoon vanilla
½ tablespoon baking powder
½ tablespoon baking soda
½ teaspoon salt
3 cups sugar
6 cups flour
1 heaping tablespoon mayonnaise (always added to our bread recipes to adjust for high altitude)

Topping
1 cup brown sugar

3 teaspoons cinnamon
$\frac{1}{2}$ cup chopped nuts

Mix eggs, oil, sour cream and vanilla (and mayonnaise, if using). Add the baking powder, baking soda, salt and sugar to the flour. Add flour mixture to the wet mixture a little at a time, until thoroughly combined.

Spray a 12 x 18 deep baking pan with vegetable oil. Put half the batter in the pan and cover with half the topping. Add the other half batter to pan and stir 1 cup of jam into top batter gently with a fork. Top with the rest of the topping. Bake at 350 degrees for 1 hour and 20 minutes.

ROCHESTER HOTEL, DURANGO

Oatmeal Scones

1 cup white flour
¾ cup whole wheat flour
1½ teaspoons baking powder
¾ teaspoon baking soda
½ teaspoon salt
⅔ cup sugar
¾ cup butter (1½ sticks)
1⅔ cups old-fashioned rolled oats
1 cup buttermilk
1 egg, beaten
1 tablespoon sugar

Preheat oven to 375 degrees Fahrenheit. Lightly grease a cookie sheet.

Into a Cuisinart basin, put flour, baking powder, baking soda, salt and sugar. Mix, and then add butter, blending until mixture resembles coarse meal. Stir in oats and buttermilk. Continue stirring until it forms a sticky but manageable dough. On floured surface, knead dough gently 6 times and roll out into a 1-inch-thick round.

With a 1½-inch round cutter dipped in flour, cut out as many rounds as possible. Place cut outs on a greased cookie sheet. Gather scraps into a ball, re-roll and cut new rounds. Brush scones gently with beaten egg and sprinkle with sugar.

Bake for 20 minutes on middle rack of the oven or until golden brown.

The Strater Hotel, Durango

Strater Hotel Posole (In-House Recipe)

Yield: Serves 6 to 10 people.
Posole soup is a popular dish in New Mexico and old Mexico for breakfast, lunch or dinner and reportedly a good cure for "the morning after."

2 pounds pork loin (cubed or diced; chicken can be used)
2 each small cans of hominy (more if desired)
1 each yellow onion (small diced)
1 pint mild bueno red chili
2 teaspoon oregano (more if desired)
3 ounces chicken base
½ gallon water
2 tablespoons cumin
Salt and Pepper to taste

Sear meat until it is cooked enough to shred. Combine hominy, onion, red chili, oregano, chicken base, water and cumin. Bring to boil and simmer for 20 minutes. Season to taste with salt and pepper.

Appendix B

DIRECTORY

HOTELS	TOWN	PAGE
Adams Hotel	Denver	24
Adams Hotel	Grand Lake	131, 132
Adelphia Hotel	Trinidad	97
The Alamo Hotel	Colorado Springs	102
Alamo Hotel	Denver	24
Albany Hotel	Boulder	37
Albany Hotel	Denver	24
Albany Hotel	Newcastle	175
Albany Hotel	Wild Horse	13
Aldine Hotel	Denver	25
Alta Vista Hotel	Colorado Springs	102
Alvord House	Denver	25
Alvord House	Golden	56, 57
American Hotel	Pagosa Springs	113
American House	Buena Vista	115
American House	Denver	25
American House	Minturn	126
Ames Hotel	Ames	199, 200
The Antlers Hotel	Colorado Springs	102, 103
Antlers Hotel	Nederland	41
Antlers Hotel	Yampa	159, 160
Arlington Hotel	Manitou Springs	86
Arlington House	Breckenridge	162
Arlington House	Denver	25

HOTELS	TOWN	PAGE
Artist's View	Evergreen	54
Astor House Hotel	Golden	56
Aunt Kate Hotel	Seibert	15
Auntie Stanes Mess Hall and Hotel	Fort Collins	67
Avenue Hotel	Golden	57
B Street Hotel	Loveland	68
Babcock Inn	Evergreen	54
Badger Hotel	Alpine	115
The Baker	Craig	185
Bald Pate Inn	Estes Park	60
Barker House	Manitou Springs	86
Bartz Hotel	Steamboat Springs	158
Bassick Hotel	Querida	81
The Batione	Denver	25
Batterson House	Fort Collins	67
Beaumont Hotel	Ouray	188–190
Beebee House Hotel	Idaho Spring	48
Beebee House	Manitou Springs	86
Bellevue House	Manitou Springs	87
The Belvoir	Denver	25
Bergh Hotel	Fairplay	150
Berthoud Pass Inn	Berthoud Pass	129
Billings Ranch	Lyons	40
The Binford	Denver	25
Black Cañon Hotel	Cimarron	187
Blake Hotel	La Jara	123
Blanca Hotel	Monte Vista	157
Bon Ton Hotel	Salida	120
Bonnieblink	Manitou Springs	87
Boulder House	Boulder	37
The Bowen	Boulder	39
Brandon Hotel	Brandon	14
The BROADMOOR	Colorado Springs	103–106
Broadwell Hotel	Denver	25
Broadwell House	Alamosa	112
Brook Forest Inn	Evergreen	54, 55
The Bross Hotel	Paonia	167, 168, 208, 209
The Brown Palace	Denver	25–27, 210–212
Brown's Mountain House	Nederland	41

Directory

Directory

Directory

Appendix B

Hotels	Town	Page
Hotel Cranford	Grand Junction	184
Hotel Crest	Denver	27
Hotel Crestone	Crestone	161
Hotel Denver	Glenwood Springs	174
Hotel de Paris	Georgetown	45, 46
Hotel Delano	De Beque	183
Hotel El Rio	Del Norte	156
Hotel Elliot	Ophir	201
Hotel Evans Spruce Lodge	Berthoud Pass	129
Hotel Gilmore	Trinidad	98
Hotel Glenwood	Glenwood Springs	174
Hotel Great Northern	Denver	28
Hotel Hawley	Wolcott	128
Hotel Hudson	Buffalo Creek	52
Hotel Jerome	Aspen	153, 154
Hotel Lemmon	Mancos	186
Hotel Maine	Pueblo	108
Hotel McClancy	Ward	42, 43
Hotel Metropole	Denver	29
Hotel Metropole	Victor	73
Motel Midland	Denver	30
Hotel Monte Cristo	Salida	120
Hotel Park	Fruita	183
Hotel Plaza	Denver	31
Hotel Ramona	Cascade	84
Hotel Rhode	Rico	169
Hotel Rollinsville	Rollinsville	52
Hotel St. Nicholas	Cripple Creek	71
Hotel Union	Greeley	76
Hotel Vail	Pueblo	108
Hotel Vendome	Leadville	142
Hotel Victor	Denver	33
Hotel Victor	Victor	73–75
Hotel Yampa	Yampa	160
Hotel Windsor	Leadville	142
Hunter Hotel	Monte Vista	157
Imperial Hotel	Cripple Creek	71
Imperial Hotel	Longmont	77
Imperial Hotel	Pueblo	108
Insmont Hotel	Insmont	151, 152
Inter-Laken	Twin Lakes	42

Directory

Directory

HOTELS	TOWN	PAGE
Pine Log Inn	El Dora Lake	39
Pfaltzgraff Hotel	Wild Horse	13
Platoro Hotel	Platoro	124
Plaza Hotel	Colorado Springs	107
Plymouth Place Hotel	Denver	31
Poncha Springs Hotel	Poncha Springs	117, 118
Portland Hotel	Cripple Creek	72
Portland Hotel:	Idaho Springs	48
Poudre Valley Hotel	Fort Collins	68
Powell House	Silver Cliff	80
Powell House	Westcliffe	80, 81
Princeton Hotel	Buena Vista	117
Pueblo House	Lake City	137
Quartzite Hotel	Red Cliff	127
Rainbow Hotel	Sapinero	136
Red Crags Lodge	Manitou Springs	90
Red Elk Hotel	Colorado Springs	107
Redstone Inn	Redstone	155
Revere Hotel	Denver	32
Riverside Hotel	Hot Sulphur Springs	132
The Rochester Hotel	Durango	179, 180, 222
Rock Island Hotel	Colorado Springs	107
Rock Island Hotel	Florence	95
Rockland Hotel	Palmer Lake	91
Rocky Mountain House	Montezuma	164
The Royal	Craig	185
Royal Hotel	Pueblo	108
Royal Hotel	Yampa	160
Rupp Hotel	Monument	90
The Rustic Hotel	Estes Park	65
Rustic Hotel	Grand Lake	132
Rustic House	Fort Collins	68
Ruxton Hotel	Manitou Springs	90
St. Charles Hotel	Alamosa	112
St. Clair Hotel	Salida	120
St. Cloud Hotel	Cañon City	94
St. Cloud Hotel	Silver Cliff	81
St. Elmo Hotel	Denver	32
St. Elmo Hotel	Ouray	190–192
St. Francis Hotel	Denver	32

Directory

APPENDIX B

HOTELS	TOWN	PAGE
Strontia Springs Hotel	Deansbury/	
	Strontia Springs	53
Stout Hotel	Stout	69
Summit House	Montezuma	164
Sunny Side Hotel	Manitou Springs	90
Sweetwater Hotel	Gypsum	125
Sylvania Hotel	Denver	33
Tabor Grand Hotel	Leadville	141, 142
Tedmon House	Fort Collins	68
Teller House	Central City	51
Terrace Hotel	Green Mountain Falls	85
Throckmorton Villa	Grand Lake	132
Timberline Hotel	Estes Park	66
Timberline Hotel	Holy Cross City	125, 126
Toll Inn	Tolland	52
Toltec Hotel	Trinidad	99
Travelers Hotel	Gypsum	125
Trinidad Hotel	Trinidad	99
Trocadero Hotel	Idaho Springs	49
Troutdale Hotel	Evergreen	55, 56
Turret Hotel	Turret	121
Twentieth Century House	Placerville	201
Twin Lakes Hotel	Walsenburg	96
Ulin Hotel	Gypsum	125
Union Stock Yards Hotel	Denver	33
The Vallejo	Denver	33
Valley View Hot Springs	Villa Grove	161
Victor Hotel	Ophir	201
Victoria Hotel	Alamosa	112
Victoria Hotel	Pueblo	108
Victoria Hotel	Telluride	204
Vulcan Hotel	Cebolla Hot Springs	133
The Waddell	Denver	33
Walker House	Silverton	198
Wall Street Hotel	Wall Street	42
Walsenburg House	Walsenburg	96
Ward's Hotel	Denver	33
Warren House	Breckenridge	163
Welch's Resort	Lyons	40
Wellington Hotel	Wellington Lake	58
Wellsville Springs	Salida	120

Directory

HOTELS	TOWN	PAGE
Westcliffe Hotel	Westcliffe	82
Western Hotel	Denver	33
Western Hotel	Ouray	191, 192
Whitewater Hotel	Whitewater	185
The Willows	Hot Sulphur Springs	132
Wilson Hotel	Ouray	192
Wilson House	Rye	109
Wind River Lodge	Estes Park	66
Windsor Hotel	Aspen	156
Windsor Hotel	Denver	34–35
Windsor Hotel	Del Norte	156
Woodland Hotel	Woodland Park	75
Woods Hotel	Walden	138
Woodson House	Ophir	201
Wolff Hotel	Westcliffe	82
Yates House Hotel	Georgetown	46
Zang's Hotel	Creede	144–146

About the Author

B orn a native Tennessean, Alexandra Walker Clark grew up in Colorado. As an adult, she returned to her adopted home state and worked as a reporter for Denver newspapers. Childhood hikes through mountains and canyons with her father, a photographer, left such indelible memories that its vast, sweeping plains and iconic mountains still remain Clark's spiritual home. In the late 1950s, Clark's grandfather, Tennessee naturalist and author Robert Sparks Walker, traveled west to visit his family, and sought out the widowed Mrs. Enos Mills in Estes Park. A small child at the time, Clark still remembers that meeting of two great minds sharing like-minded philosophy and love of nature as they stood in the strong Colorado sun, reminiscing about Enos Mills beneath the majesty of his beloved Long's Peak.

Clark, an avid traveler, is a lover of historic architecture and seeks to stay in old hotels. She and her husband owned three bed-and-breakfasts while raising a family. Sometimes their small children were rushed to the attic so their rooms could be rented for the night. Such recollections colored research of the lesser hotels, providing insight into rustic innkeeping in Colorado's early days. Some of these rough buildings, purporting to be hotels over a century ago, would be laughed at today. But there were also fantastic, extravagant structures that must have seemed like castles in the wilderness. While it is sad to realize how many of the grand hotels have perished, those that survive are treasures to be preserved for future generations.